THE LEGACY OF
WINNICOTT

THE LEGACY OF
WINNICOTT
Essays on Infant
and Child Mental Health

edited by
Brett Kahr

Foreword by
Patrick Casement

KARNAC
LONDON   NEW YORK

First published in 2002 by
H. Karnac (Books) Ltd.
6 Pembroke Buildings, London NW10 6RE
Reprinted 2003

British Library Cataloguing in Publication Data

A C.I.P. for this book is available from the British Library

ISBN 1 85575 236 0

10 9 8 7 6 5 4 3 2 1

Edited, designed, and produced by Communication Crafts

Printed and bound in Great Britain by Biddles Ltd,
Guildford and King's Lynn

www.karnacbooks.com

Dedicated to the memory of
Dr Donald Woods Winnicott (1896–1971),
and for
Dr Ved Varma,
for their pioneering contributions to
the development of child psychology in Great Britain

In our culture at the present time we are reaping the rewards of an era in which every effort is being made to give children, at any rate, the beginnings of a sense of freedom to exist in their own right.

Winnicott, 1969b, p. 232

CONTENTS

ACKNOWLEDGEMENTS

Shortly before Donald Winnicott's death on 25 January 1971, Dr Ved Varma, an educational psychologist working in London, approached Winnicott with the intention of editing a Festschrift in his honour. Varma had long admired Winnicott's contributions to the study of child psychology, and he sent the aged and ailing psychoanalyst an outline for a book entitled *Child Psychiatry Today*, which would pay tribute to Donald Winnicott's discoveries. In his synopsis, Varma suggested many excellent British mental health professionals as chapter writers, including not only Winnicott himself, but also such noted figures as Dr John Bowlby, Mrs Dorothy Burlingham, Dr Siegmund Foulkes, Miss Anna Freud, Professor Sir Aubrey Lewis, Dr Agnes Main, Dr David Malan, Dr Joseph Sandler, Dr William Sargant, and Professor Erwin Stengel. Winnicott expressed considerable interest in the project, but he ultimately demurred, in part because he felt that it might not be appropriate for colleagues to celebrate his work in such an overt manner during his own lifetime.

Ved Varma has since gone on to edit a great many readable and useful books on a wide variety of mental health topics (e.g. Varma, 1974, 1993), but he never realized his original plans for a Winnicott commemorative volume. In 1994, I had the opportunity to interview Dr Varma as part of my ongoing biographical research about Donald Winnicott (Kahr, 1996a), and during the course of our meetings, we decided that the time would now be ripe to reactivate plans for a book of papers dedicated to the undisputed pioneer of infant mental health studies. As the centenary of Winnicott's birth loomed large, Dr Varma and I decided to commission a set of new essays from contemporary workers to mark Winnicott's one hundredth year. Unfortunately, poor health had prevented Dr Varma from participating in the subsequent commissioning and editing of the contributions, thus delaying our project somewhat, but he must receive all due credit for the original idea; and I have dedicated this centenary volume to the memory of Donald Winnicott and to Ved Varma, for their continuous commitment to the study and welfare of young children.

I wish to extend my very warmest thanks to the many skilled and thoughtful contributors for having produced such lucid and informative papers with alacrity, in spite of their busy professional timetables. I also want to extend my thanks to Mr Leo Abse, former chairman of the Winnicott Clinic of Psychotherapy, for his particular encouragement of this project.

I owe immense gratitude to Mr Eric Koops, the current chairman of the Winnicott Clinic of Psychotherapy, and to his fellow Trustees, and to the Clinic secretary, Mrs Frances Hawkins, for their successful efforts in establishing the Winnicott Clinic Senior Research Fellowship in Psychotherapy in collaboration with the School of Psychotherapy and Counselling at Regent's College, under the Deanship of Professor Ernesto Spinelli. I am very honoured to have been selected as the inaugural Winnicott Clinic Senior Research Fellow, and I completed the final editorial work of this commemorative volume under the auspices of this fellowship.

I have used small segments of Winnicott's unpublished correspondence in my introductory essay. I wish to extend my appreciation to Mr Mark Paterson of Sigmund Freud Copyrights and to the Winnicott Trust for their permission to use Winnicott's original words, and to Dr George Makari and Mr Paul Bunten of the Archives of Psychiatry at the Oskar Diethelm Library of the History of Psychiatry at the Cornell Medical Center, in New York City, for their expert custodianship of the Donald W. Winnicott Papers and for their many scholarly courtesies over the years.

As always, I offer my deep appreciation to all the staff at Karnac, the most convivial and efficient of publishers and booksellers. Mr Cesare Sacerdoti, the emeritus publisher, supported this project unflaggingly during its long gestation, and this volume bears all the hallmarks of his unique, scholarly attention to both breadth and detail; I remain forever indebted to him for his confidence, and for his appreciation of the value of Donald Winnicott's lasting contributions. Mr Graham Sleight, then at Karnac, expended a great deal of time and energy in the editing of this complex multiauthored book, made many crucial suggestions concerning structure and organization, and brought much clarity and readability to some of the more unwieldy paragraphs. Mr Eric King and Mrs Klara King undertook the laborious task of copy-editing and typesetting with their famous cheerfulness and with unparalleled accuracy. The many highly intelligent Karnac staff members have assisted on so many occasions, too numerous count, for which I offer further thanks. Dr Michael Moskowitz, the current publisher of H. Karnac Books, and his extremely able team have inherited this project and have executed all their responsibilities with terrific professionalism and with great enthusiasm, for which I thank them.

I doubt that I could have edited this book without the assistance and the interest of my students and colleagues in the School of Psychotherapy and Counselling at Regent's College, who have tolerated and encouraged my ongoing Winnicott research. Without the administrative support of Ms Geraldine Creaven, Ms Megan Fowler, Ms Caroline Gittins, Mr Ian Jones-Healey, and Mrs Teresa Norman, in particular—my continuously generous computer advisers and staunch advocates in so many other ways—I could not have completed the final editorial work.

Brett Kahr
Regent's Park, London
September 2002

CONTRIBUTORS

STELLA ACQUARONE is a psychologist and a child psychotherapist and adult psychotherapist. She is director of the Parent Infant Clinic in London, and director of the School of Infant Mental Health. She also coordinates a psychotherapeutic service for emotionally disturbed infants, based in the National Health Service. She is the author of the forthcoming book *Parent–Infant Psychotherapy: A Handbook for Parents and Professionals.*

E. JAMES ANTHONY is a child psychiatrist and psychoanalyst. He works as director of Child and Adolescent Psychotherapy at the Chestnut Lodge Clinic in Rockville, Maryland. He is also Clinical Professor of Psychiatry and Behavior at the George Washington University Medical School. His many books include *Parenthood: Its Psychology and Psychopathology,* co-edited with Therese Benedek, to which the late Donald Winnicott contributed a chapter.

PATRICK CASEMENT is a training analyst and supervising analyst at the Institute of Psycho-Analysis in London and a psychoanalyst in private practice. Trained originally in social work and in psychoanalytic psychotherapy, he is a graduate of the British Association of Psychotherapists, and of the Institute of Psycho-Analysis. He is a Member of the British Psycho-Analytical Society, and the author of *On Learning from the Patient*, and *Further Learning from the Patient*, as well as numerous papers and book chapters. His latest book is entitled *Learning from Our Mistakes: Beyond Dogma in Psychoanalysis and Psychotherapy*.

LLOYD DEMAUSE is the director of the Institute for Psychohistory in New York, and editor of the *Journal of Psychohistory*, as well as founding president of the International Psychohistorical Association. His many books include *The History of Childhood*, *The New Psychohistory*, *Foundations of Psychohistory*, *Reagan's America*, as well as a forthcoming study of the impact of child abuse on Western civilization, entitled *The Emotional Life of Nations*.

SIRA DERMEN trained as a child psychotherapist at the Tavistock Clinic and subsequently qualified as a psychoanalyst from the Institute of Psycho-Analysis. She currently works as principal adult psychotherapist at the Portman Clinic and as a psychoanalyst in private practice in London. She is a member of the British Psycho-Analytical Society and the British Confederation of Psychotherapists, and a training analyst at the Institute of Psycho-Analysis.

HUGH GEE is a training analyst at the Society of Analytical Psychology, where he trained as a Jungian analyst, and a training therapist with the Jungian Analytic Section of the British Association of Psychotherapists. He is also a member of the British Confederation of Psychotherapists. He has written many papers, including "Developing insight through supervision : relating, then defining".

DAVID HOLBROOK is an emeritus fellow of Downing College of the University of Cambridge, having served as director of studies in English over many years. He is the author or editor of numerous books, including *English for the Rejected: Training Literacy in the Lower Streams of the Secondary School*, *The Case Against Pornography*, and *Creativity and Popular Culture*.

ALASDAIR HONEYMAN trained initially as a paediatrician at the Royal London Hospital, and he currently works as a registrar in general practice at the Stockwell Group Practice in London. He is a member of the Royal College of Physicians.

JULIET HOPKINS is a child psychotherapist and an adult psychotherapist working in private practice. She served for many years as a consultant child psychotherapist in the Child and Family Department at the Tavistock Clinic in London. Dr Hopkins is also a member of the Advisory Committee of the Winnicott Research Unit at the University of Cambridge, and she holds membership in the Association of Child Psychotherapists, the British Association of Psychotherapists, and the British Confederation of Psychotherapists.

BRETT KAHR works as senior lecturer in psychotherapy in the School of Psychotherapy and Counselling at Regent's College in London and is currently the Winnicott Clinic Senior Research Fellow in Psychotherapy, sponsored by the Winnicott Clinic of Psychotherapy, in association with Regent's College. He is the author of *D. W. Winnicott: A Biographical Portrait*, published by Karnac Books and International Universities Press, which won the Gradiva Award for Biography from the National Association for the Advancement of Psychoanalysis and the American Board for Accreditation in Psychoanalysis. He is the editor of *Forensic Psychotherapy and Psychopathology: Winnicottian Perspectives*, published by Karnac Books, as well as the series editor for the Karnac Books Forensic Psychotherapy Monograph Series. He is a patron of the Squiggle Foundation, and adviser to the Winnicott Clinic of Psychotherapy. He has published a book on *Exhibitionism* in the series on "Ideas in Psychoanalysis". He is also Chair of the Professional and Public Relations Committee of the United Kingdom Council for Psychotherapy.

ROBERT LANGS works in private practice as a psychoanalyst and is an Honorary Visiting Fellow at the School of Psychotherapy and Counselling at Regent's College in London. He has written more than 35 books on psychoanalysis and psychotherapy, including *The Bipersonal Field, Doing Supervision and Being Supervised, Clinical Practice and the Architecture of the Mind, The Evolution of the Emotion-Processing Mind,* and *Death Anxiety and Clinical Practice.*

SUSIE ORBACH trained as a social worker and as an adult psychotherapist. She is visiting professor at the Gender Studies Institute of the London School of Economics and Political Science of the University of London, and she maintains a private practice in psychoanalytic psychotherapy in London. Professor Orbach is the founder of the Women's Therapy Centre in London and of the Women's Therapy Center Institute in New York. Her many books include *Fat Is a Feminist Issue, Hunger Strike: The Anorectic's Struggle as a Metaphor for Our Time, What's Really Going on Here?, The Impossibility of Sex,* and *Towards Emotional Literacy.* She writes a regular column on mental health and emotional literacy for *The Guardian* newspaper. Most recently, she published the best-seller, *Susie Orbach on Eating.*

PAUL ROAZEN is professor of social and political science at York University in Ontario, Canada, and one of the leading experts in the history of psychoanalysis, best known for his landmark book, *Freud and His Followers.* His other books include *Helene Deutsch: A Psychoanalyst's Life, Encountering Freud: The Politics and Histories of Psychoanalysis, Meeting Freud's Family, How Freud Worked: First-Hand Accounts by Patients,* and *The Historiography of Psychoanalysis.* He has also edited two volumes of collected papers by Helene Deutsch.

JUDITH TROWELL is a child psychiatrist, psychoanalyst, and child psychoanalyst, having trained at the Institute of Psycho-Analysis in London. Dr Trowell works as Consultant Child Psychiatrist in the Child and Family Department of the Tavistock Clinic, in London, and has served as the former chair of the Child and Family Department as well. She is also a Fellow of the Royal College of Psychiatrists and an Honorary Senior Lecturer at the Royal Free and University College Hospital School of Medicine, and she has written *Understanding Your 3 Year Old,* and edited *The Emotional Needs of Young Children and Their Families: Using Psychoanalytic Ideas in the Community,* with Marion Bower. Most recently, she has co-edited *The Importance of Fathers: A Psychoanalytic Re-Evaluation,* with Alicia Etchegoyen. She is also a trustee of the Winnicott Trust and the Chair of Young Minds. In addition, she is Vice-Chair of the Camden Area Child Protection Committee.

PREFACE

In 1966, the British Psycho-Analytical Society hosted a lavish and successful party at its London headquarters to celebrate the seventieth birthday of Dr Donald Woods Winnicott, one of the organization's most revered members. Mrs Enid Balint, one of Winnicott's former analysands and a distinguished practitioner in her own right, helped to organize the event. Although Winnicott enjoyed the party immensely, he harboured no omnipotent or grandiose illusions that his colleagues had arranged the gala evening for his benefit alone. On 8 December 1966, Winnicott wrote a letter to Dr Michael Balint, the husband of Enid Balint, remarking: "It seemed at the time that the Society wanted to have a party and to use my birthday as an excuse but of course in the end it turned out to be a party for me" (Winnicott, 1966c). The fête at Mansfield House served not only to mark Winnicott's birthday, but also as a means of bringing colleagues together, to benefit from one another's company, and to play.

An immensely social man in his own right, Donald Winnicott devoted much of his life to the task of uniting people. For instance, as an undergraduate student at the University of Cambridge, he organized a troop of boy scouts (Winnicott, 1968c). Years later, as a fully qualified psychoanalyst, Winnicott laboured to bring troubled families together, arguing that babies require the support of caretaking mothers and that mothers require the support of husbands and fathers (cf. Winnicott, 1944a).

In the admirable spirit of Winnicottian inclusiveness, I have attempted to assemble a collection of essays and reminiscences that not only pay tribute to Donald Winnicott more than one hundred years after his birth, but will also function as a means of presenting the work of a group of thoughtful, intelligent clinicians and scholars, all of whom I admire immensely, both professionally and personally, between the covers of one single, usable volume. This book, *The Legacy of Winnicott: Essays on Infant and Child Mental Health*, will serve not only as a belated birthday gift for Donald Winnicott, but also as a compilation of high-quality essays for professionals and for students in the mental health field, offering a glimpse into the modern elaboration of Winnicott's bountiful ideas.

Apart from Sigmund Freud, no other substantial figure in the history of psychoanalysis or dynamic psychotherapy has written as much as Winnicott has done, and no one else has lectured as widely and as frequently as Winnicott, speaking not only to groups of psychoanalysts and child psychiatrists, but also to parents, child care workers, midwives, nurses, probation officers, adoption workers, borstal workers, social workers, and teachers. In doing so, Winnicott attempted to forge a brand of psychoanalysis that would not only enrich his colleagues, but which would reach and enhance those in cognate disciplines, not least those hard-working, unpaid professionals called *mothers* and *fathers*. Winnicott fervently believed that psychological knowledge should be shared, and he endeavoured to write in clear prose, eschewing the abundant footnotes and bibliographical references so endemic in academic writing. As editor of *The Legacy of Winnicott: Essays on Infant and Child Mental Health*, I strove to choose contributors who not only think well, but can communicate with ease and with clarity, in the hope that many of the important clinical observations contained herein can be absorbed by a wider audience.

FOREWORD

Patrick Casement

I am delighted to have been asked to contribute a Foreword to this Festschrift to Winnicott, celebrating his life-work and vision. In this brief appreciation of Winnicott, as my introduction to this volume, I wish first to highlight some of his contributions that particularly illustrate the originality of his thought, and then I shall focus on some of his indirect as well as direct contributions to psychoanalytic technique.

Like many others who met Winnicott, I too have "my" Winnicott. This is based upon my having heard him speak (on too few occasions) and meeting him in person only once. But, much more than this, I have "met" Winnicott more intimately and frequently in my consulting-room, in working with patients. It has been through following *them* that I have so often been led back to Winnicott, with my understanding of what he had written becoming both extended and deepened. And it has been my recurring experience that, even though Winnicott's writing can at times be rather obscure and difficult to follow, it is in meeting clinical phenomena similar to those that he has described, that we can most often come to understand what he had been trying to communicate. It is by

re-finding Winnicott, clinically, that we can best understand him—
or so I have found.

In my opinion, the value of Winnicott's ideas is not so much in
being able to apply them as in *looking where he looked* and *seeing for
ourselves* something of what he has observed and commented on.
And what we see when we follow the spotlight of his vision, will
sometimes be much more than just a confirmation of his views, for
it is enriched by the individuality of the persons with whom we are
dealing. Winnicott's vision was never a closed system, to be applied or to be proved by others. It was essentially and always open,
responsive to the newness in each person alongside anything that
might also be familiar from his observation of others. For Winnicott's passion was in following his patients, not in leading them.

In relation to so many areas of life, Winnicott showed his originality and genius in seeing things differently. For example, one
concept of his that is, in my opinion, too little referred to is that
of the antisocial tendency, a state of mind that he regarded as
pre-delinquent (Winnicott, 1956). To paraphrase Winnicott, he observed that when a child has been deprived of something essential
to security and growth and has been deprived of this for too long,
the child may go in search of this symbolically, through stealing,
when hopeful. Who other than Winnicott would have been able to
recognize that thrust of unconscious hope, even in stealing?

Winnicott also recognized that in destructiveness, too—the
other form of the antisocial tendency that he noted—a child may
similarly be in search of something missing: a containment that can
allow for a fuller aliveness than had previously been safely possible. Frequently, the parents or other caregivers have collapsed or
retaliated when a child has been seeking to explore the full potential of his or her energetic vitality. Winnicott recognized that such
a child is often in search of an "other" who is able to help this
potentially destructive energy to become manageable, rather than
still being experienced as too much for adults to manage and therefore, inevitably, too much also for the child.

The central point in each of these forms of the antisocial tendency is that the environment should come to meet "the moment of
hope" (Winnicott, 1956, p. 309). And when the unconscious hope in
this *is* met, then the need expressed in the behaviour can be at-

tended to, and the antisocial behaviour may begin to become redundant, having served its unconscious purpose. But if the moment of hope is *not* met, then we can expect the antisocial behaviour to progress further into delinquency, the child settling for some gratification in stealing, or in the excitement of destructive behaviour, to distract from the disappointment that a deeper need has remained unrecognized and unmet. But these replacement behaviours are likely to become addictive as they can never make up for the failure of the environment to meet those needs that had earlier been expressed in the antisocial tendency.

I have chosen to comment, in particular, on the antisocial tendency, because it illustrates so well the genius of Winnicott's observation and thinking. For similar reasons I would like to mention his ideas on the fear of breakdown (Winnicott, 1974). Typically, Winnicott was able to recognize in this that *the thing feared has already happened*. But if early trauma has been beyond the capacity of the immature mind to survive without the risk of going to pieces or disintegrating, then the trauma may be split off in the mind as if it had not yet happened, or, to be more specific, as if the ego had not been in the experience. The mind then dreads ever joining up with the experience from which it has remained defensively absent—the dread being that the postponed disintegration might still happen.

Winnicott (1955, p. 20) also points out that, when trauma has been split off in this way, the details of the trauma are "frozen" in the mind, with the unconscious hope that a time may come when it could be possible to unfreeze the trauma, with more adequate help available to hold the person through a joining up with what has factually been known to have happened but emotionally has not yet been fully experienced. Only then can the feared breakdown be sufficiently encountered and experienced in the present, and only then can it begin to attain a past tense, now as having happened.

In relation to this, Winnicott also observed that the details of the trauma, frozen in the mind, are catalogued, and it is extraordinary how much of that detail comes to be available when the trauma is unfrozen from the unconscious and is experienced more fully in the present of an analysis. [I was greatly helped by Winnicott's thinking here when I had the privilege of working with such a

traumatized patient; the details of that process of "unfreezing" I
have since been permitted to publish (Casement, 1985)].

These are just a few examples of Winnicott's profoundly per-
ceptive understanding of clinical phenomena that can have a far-
reaching value in the clinical field. But in many ways Winnicott
also illumined familiar concepts with fresh vision. This revolution
of thinking, so typical of Winnicott, has been well described by
Goldman (1993) in the introduction to his book:

> [Winnicott] . . . reframed words to arrive at innovative con-
> cepts, often turning old ones upside-down. [He] turned around
> the . . . term "depersonalization" to fashion his concept of
> "personalization." "Integration" suggested to him the idea
> of "unintegration." "Ruthlessness," in Winnicott's hands, was
> contrasted with a "stage of ruth." Winnicott [also] loved stand-
> ing classical ideas on their head! Where Freud saw psycho-
> analysis as a way of freeing people from illusions, Winnicott
> emphasised the freedom to create and enjoy illusions. Whereas
> classical technique centred on the value of interpretations,
> Winnicott pointed to the value of not interpreting. Whereas
> classical theory had explored the infantile fear of being alone,
> Winnicott spoke of the mature capacity to be alone. Regression,
> rather than being pathological in that it provides a surfeit of
> infantile gratification, becomes, in Winnicott's hands, a process
> of healing through a search for missing experiences. Psychoso-
> matic illness was not a withdrawal of interest from the outside
> world, as classical theory claimed, but an attempt to rediscover
> one's own body. [Goldman, 1993, p. xxiii]

I wish to turn to matters relating more specifically to psychoanalytic technique. Although Winnicott had supervision with Melanie
Klein and admired much of her work, he had problems with how
her ideas were being applied. In particular, he could not stand the
certainty with which her followers represented her understanding,
nor could he stand it when some of them became what he referred
to as "her proselytizers". It was not for him either to be a follower
or to seek followers. Even though Winnicott has been falsely cred-
ited with being one of the founders of the Middle Group or the
Independent Group within the British Psycho-Analytical Society,
he never wished to belong to a group, let alone to found one.
Instead of telling people how to think or how to work, Winnicott

pointed towards where they might look. Then, maybe, they might see clinical phenomena illumined by a light similar to that which had continued to inspire him.

In following his patients, Winnicott encouraged others likewise to follow theirs. It was particularly important for him *not* to lead, for it was a patient's initiative, creativity, and aliveness that he regarded as most precious and which he hoped to be able to release from whatever it was that threatened to impair or to imprison it. Anathema to Winnicott was anything that might lead to compliance, to that existential death from which he most particularly hoped to be able to free those with whom he had dealings. So, from his work with mothers and infants and children of all ages, Winnicott became convinced of the damage that could be done to the budding psyche by the "impingements" of a mother and other carers.

Among Winnicott's many inspired observations to do with impingement were the two uses of the spatula: (1) that for which it had been designed, to be pushed down a throat for depressing the tongue, and (2), if left within reach, for a child to discover and to play with (Winnicott, 1941). As many people now know, Winnicott noticed that a healthy infant would resist having this foreign object thrust into the mouth, whereas a less healthy, compliant child might allow this. Equally, when it was left in sight, a healthy child would begin to invest this shiny new object with interest, eventually reaching for it and using it in the service of play.

This now familiar observation of infants in a set situation (Winnicott, 1941) lends itself naturally to an extension into the realm of psychoanalytic technique. For there, too, the analyst can be experienced by the patient in either way: as a spatula that is frequently *thrust down the throat of the patient*, as with interpretations of assumed transference, whether or not the patient can make use of them; *or*, quite differently, as an unobtrusive presence, to be gradually invested by the patient with significance, then *to be explored*, and at times *to be played with*, as by a healthy infant allowed time to discover the spatula. Herein is the area of play that Winnicott regarded as so essential to any creative psychotherapy or analysis. And he said of this: "Interpretation when the patient has no capacity to play is simply not useful, or causes confusion" (Winnicott, 1968a, p. 597).

Likewise, with the squiggle game, Winnicott discovered a technique that also has its relevance in the sphere of interpretation. He would offer a shape for a child to make something of it, or the child would offer a shape to Winnicott for him to make something of it. Here, too, without emphasizing the parallels to analytic work, Winnicott lets us discover these parallels for ourselves. In particular, he cautions that "Interpretation outside the ripeness of the material is indoctrination and produces compliance" (Winnicott, 1968a, p. 597).

We can see here the value, when appropriate, in making incomplete interpretations, inviting the patient to make something of them, rather than attempting either to monopolize insight or to define meaning for a patient. Winnicott also highlighted the value of not knowing, not as ignorance, but as a positive hesitation with regard to insight, and provisional understanding that it be kept open for further development, as much by the patient as by the analyst. He clearly recognized that a patient's truth was to be found from within the patient. It was not something that could be given by the analyst.

And, in his own use of interpretation, Winnicott eventually came to see the importance of using this much more sparingly. In a now very familiar statement, he said:

> It appals me to think how much deep change I have prevented or delayed in patients in a certain classification category by my personal need to interpret. If only we can wait, the patient arrives at understanding creatively and with immense joy, and I now enjoy this joy more than I used to enjoy the sense of having been clever. I think I interpret mainly to let the patient know the limits of my understanding. The principle is that it is the patient and only the patient who has the answers. We may or may not enable him or her to be able to encompass what is known or become aware of it with acceptance. [Winnicott, 1969a, p. 711]

In all of this, Winnicott was careful to avoid impingements upon a patient—anything that could prompt a patient to get lost in compliance. And, in my opinion, he understood here, as clearly as anyone, the unique spirit and opportunity of psychoanalysis: that it has the potential to free the mind from what has previously kept it imprisoned. And what could be more imprisoning than the entrapment of a false self, so often developed in response to the pressures and expectations of others? So it is of crucial importance that a patient, particularly one given to compliance, should be able to find within the psychoanalytic relationship a freedom from those pressures to comply. In this, Winnicott held up a light that challenges all of us with regard to the environment provided by the analyst.

Bearing in mind so much of what Winnicott has said about the importance of environmental provision for healthy development, it follows that much the same applies to the analytic relationship—for how can it enable healthy growth and the flowering of creativity within the patient, if the analyst becomes impinging or controlling? However much may be attributed to the analyst by the patient, based upon the patient's experience of significant others, we should never overlook the impact of the analyst as environment to a patient, for if we do not give due acknowledgement to that external reality, it can lead to confusion and mix-up in the analysis, particularly if disturbance is being attributed to the patient when a part, at least, is coming from the analyst.

One result of an analysis conducted with too much certainty on the part of the analyst is that the patient is put under pressure to choose between opposing the analyst, at the risk of that being interpreted in terms of some resistance, or in due course having to comply. The outcome of that may be either that the analysis breaks down into impasse or, in some cases, that it results in what amounts to a false-self analysis. This can be a consequence of a patient having to fit in too much with the analyst's ways of seeing things, at the cost of becoming untrue to the patient's inner core self.

Throughout Winnicott's observation of infants and his clinical work with patients, he was concerned to enable the true, inner, secret self to find a freedom to emerge more confidently, in order to develop and to grow. From that point of view, it is a tragedy when an analysis threatens to become something that seems, instead, to be controlling of the patient and controlled by the analyst. I think that we might all aim to keep this caution in mind, as none of us is entirely free from a tendency to control, to dominate, and to think that we know best. And it is ironic that the analyst is specifically placed in a position where he or she may be expected to know best! We may know some things that a patient cannot know unaided, but it behoves us to be extremely careful in how we handle the special sense of a patient that we have been trained to develop, but which we might come to treat as privileged knowledge. The analyst's assumed understanding of the patient can then so easily veer towards becoming an impingement and a pressure upon a patient to comply, even when we think that we are being careful to avoid this.

But Winnicott did not advocate any limp idea of simply following a patient, to the point of letting him or her be in control of the analysis all the time. It was mainly at times of regression when Winnicott advocated the need to allow the analysis to be conducted "within the omnipotence of the patient", and the late Dr Martin James, a psychoanalyst, likewise recommended this at the start of some analyses (private communication). But, as with the development of an infant, it becomes necessary that the mother or the analyst also recognize those occasions when what is needed— as opposed to what may be demanded—is to respond with a progressive failure to adapt (Winnicott, 1963b).

Also, there are times when a patient will seek out opportunities for confrontation, as in adolescence, which Winnicott describes so tellingly in the final chapter in *Playing and Reality* (Winnicott, 1971a). There he stresses the importance of going to meet the need for confrontation, meeting it without changing colour, and surviving the attacks that, in phantasy, are to do with killing the parent. It is then crucial that the parent or analyst survives this without collapse or retaliation.

Finally, one of the most creative but also most difficult of the concepts left to us by Winnicott is that of the "The Use of an Object" (Winnicott, 1969a, 1971a). He recognized that there comes a crucial time when an infant, or a patient, needs to discover that the object (parent or analyst) has a capacity to survive the fullest attacks that belong to the patient's destruction in phantasy of the object. Prior to this, the object may be thought of as surviving only because the infant, or the patient, has continued to protect it.

This omnipotent protection of the object is like that of the sun-dancing of primitive tribes, which was relied upon to make sure that the sun would rise again each day—and it worked every time! But continuing to believe that the object remains dependent upon the magic of this protection can result in a fearful sense of responsibility for the well-being of the object. It also denies the infant/patient the benefit and security of being in the safe hands of another person who is able to survive in his or her own right—not merely because of being kept alive through omnipotent protection in phantasy by either infant or patient.

This notion of the use of an object seems to be very difficult for some people to understand, and this may be because there really is no satisfactory substitute for having been there with a patient. I have therefore remained forever grateful that I had the opportunity (described in detail in Chapter 7 of Casement, 1985) to have met with this clinical phenomenon in such clear terms. I had to ensure that I survived this, seeking such help as I needed so that I did not either collapse or retaliate. And my survival here was all the more important for this particular patient, as she had been so seriously traumatized by a sense of those she most needed failing her in both ways: either collapsing or retaliating. These two responses to her had continued to be expected by her, most particularly whenever she was most acutely needy. And it was only after getting through that prolonged and extremely difficult sequence that I, eventually, came to understand what Winnicott had meant in his description of this crucial concept, the use of an object.

I once expressed to Clare Winnicott my amazement at how precisely Winnicott had described what I had been through with my patient, during the sequences I have alluded to above. She replied: "Yes, I find that too—frequently. It is because Donald had *been there* before us."

Beyond my own playing with, and working with, some key ideas of Winnicott, I have tried to let him speak for himself. And throughout this book we can find ample evidence from the other contributors of how they, too, have been inspired by the breadth and depth of Winnicott's vision. Each of them, in individual ways, illustrates how he or she has continued to reap where he had sown. This volume will be of interest, and of value, to an audience of readers as wide as that to which Winnicott gave himself so willingly in his lifetime.

Donald Woods Winnicott: the cartographer of infancy

Brett Kahr

Winnicott's contributions

Donald Winnicott died more than thirty years ago, and since his departure many new and vibrant theoreticians have burst onto the psychoanalytical scene. Why, then, should we continue to study Winnicott's original ideas? Before Winnicott passed away in 1971, he reflected to his colleague Mrs Barbara Dockar-Drysdale that "when your work is quoted ten years after your death, by someone who does not know your name—this is fame" (quoted in Dockar-Drysdale, 1974, p. 2). Without doubt, Winnicott has achieved the status of being famous, and students invariably refer to his work on the holding environment without citing his texts as the source. And as he longed to be memorialized in some way, Winnicott would have enjoyed his current celebrity status within the psychotherapy profession (cf. Kahr, 1996a, 1996b). But many people have idealized Winnicott, such as the late psychoanalyst, Mrs Eva Rosenfeld (1970), who referred to him as "St Donald"; while others have come to know about him simply by virtue of his fame. In view of the fact that Winnicott has become increasingly a "climate of opinion" (to borrow Wystan Hugh

Auden's well-known description of Sigmund Freud), I thought it might be useful to remind readers of some of the very specific and particular achievements that have earned Winnicott an eternal place in the psychoanalytical pantheon.

Born in Plymouth, Devon, on 7 April 1896, Donald Winnicott attended school at the nearby Plymouth College, followed by four years of boarding-school at The Leys School, a Wesleyan Methodist institution in Cambridge. He received his undergraduate education at Jesus College of the University of Cambridge, and he then attended St Bartholomew's Hospital medical school in London, qualifying as a physician in 1920. From that time on, until his death more than half a century later, Dr Winnicott devoted himself to the care of the physically ill and, later, the mentally ill—first as a physician in children's medicine and then as a child psychiatrist, an adult psychoanalyst, and a child psychoanalyst. He held high offices within the British Psychological Society, the Royal Society of Medicine, and the British Psycho-Analytical Society, authoring numerous influential books and papers. The details of Winnicott's life can be studied in my book *D. W. Winnicott: A Biographical Portrait* (Kahr, 1996a), for ease of reference.

Although Winnicott worked with adults, adolescents, and children of all ages as well as with various psychopathological configurations, I regard his work on the psychology of *infancy* as Winnicott's most breathtaking and substantial contribution to Western civilization. Sigmund Freud knew, of course, that our behaviours as adults can be traced back to the vicissitudes of infantile feeding experiences, especially our relationship to the maternal breast; and years later Melanie Klein fleshed out Freud's rudimentary observations on infant breast-feeding by sketching a more complete portrait of the terrors and anxieties that plague the mind of the neonate. But in spite of Freud's paediatric experiences (Bonomi, 1994) and in spite of Klein's work with toddlers and other youngsters (e.g. Klein, 1932), neither giant could boast much formal clinical experience with actual, chronological infants. Donald Winnicott, by contrast, examined, observed, and treated literally thousands of babies as his bread-and-butter work, primarily at the Paddington Green Children's Hospital in West London, where he worked from 1923 until 1963, but also at the Queen's Hospital for Children in East London, and in his private practice.

As a result of this unusual and incomparable base of empirical data, Winnicott possessed a privileged glimpse into both the internal and the external worlds of neonates; but he also had the opportunity to learn about the psychodynamics of the mothers who cared for these infants. And furthermore, Winnicott could observe the interactions between babies and their mothers at very close range, thus permitting him to discover and to appreciate the ways in which the actual style of mothering could either impinge upon the child's development or facilitate the child's growth.

Winnicott's contributions to the psychology of infancy cannot readily be summarized, as they constitute the bulk of his corpus of writings. But one can nevertheless extract the basic discoveries and conclusions. Of greatest importance, Winnicott taught us that infants can be *interesting* individuals who are worthy of study. He encouraged the active observation of infants in his clinic as a means of obtaining diagnostic information about their psychopathology (Winnicott, 1941; cf. Kahr, 1996b). Furthermore, he observed that infants suffer from extensive primitive agonies (Winnicott, 1967), such as the fear of falling forever; and he noted that babies suffer in a state of "absolute dependence" (Winnicott, 1963b, p. 84; cf. Winnicott, 1963a), which must be greeted with reliable maternal care and protection. In other words, Winnicott helped us to appreciate that by watching babies, we can learn exactly how much infants will communicate to us both affectively and non-verbally, and that when we listen to these infantile messages, we learn only too forcefully about the vulnerability of neonates—a vulnerability that must be respected, and not abused. When adults behave sensitively to the needs of babies and strive to meet these needs, then mental health will ensue; but when adults fail their babies, varying degrees of damage will occur, resulting in different categories of mental illness, depending upon the severity of the impingement or deprivation. Stated concisely, Winnicott's greatest discovery may be the simple but vital recognition that *actual parenting produces mental health or mental illness* (Winnicott, 1960b).

Dr Winnicott also explored many other related areas of infancy, including the importance of foetal mental life, pre-natal and perinatal factors, the impact of birth experiences, and so forth (Winnicott, 1949b). Moreover, Winnicott concentrated intensively and extensively on the psychology and psychopathology of parenthood, examining the ways in which different caretaking experiences contribute to the emerging character. And, furthermore, Winnicott also wrote about the importance of parental phantasies towards their offspring, including, perhaps most vitally, the ease with which ordinary parents come to hate their children for being such dependent burdens (Winnicott, 1949a). Crucially, Winnicott recognized that parents must learn to verbalize their hatred towards babies, ideally to a psychological professional or to some other mature adult, rather than acting out the murderousness on the child in an unconscious manner. By writing about the normal human capacity for hating babies, Winnicott opened up the discourse on maternal ambivalence, thus helping mothers and other caretakers to feel less guilty about their negative affects, and thus providing an outlet for the release and abreaction of toxic emotions (cf. Parker, 1994, 1995).

Of greatest practical importance, Winnicott became the undisputed pioneer of parent–infant psychotherapy, tirelessly working with parents and with the babies themselves to understand the causes of disturbances of appetite and disturbances of sleep. His early paediatric case notes, as well as his first book, *Clinical Notes on Disorders of Childhood* (Winnicott, 1931), attest to his commitment to the unravelling of psychological and behavioural disturbances of infancy. On the basis of his work as a student of infant observation, as a theoretician of the psychology of infancy and the psychology of parents, and as an infant psychotherapist, I have come to regard Dr Donald Winnicott as the veritable *cartographer of infancy*. More than any mental health professional before or since, Winnicott drew the map of infancy as a good cartographer always does, and then he filled it in with precise details, examining the manifold ways in which a mother's ability to hold and handle her baby will influence the entire course of the infant's subsequent development.

Contemporary readers may smirk when reading Winnicott's original writings, because we now know only too well that infantile experiences do indeed serve as the substrate for adult mental health. But during the 1930s, 1940s, and 1950s few parents or professionals appreciated the vital links between early life events and subsequent psychopathology. More than anyone since Freud, Winnicott pointed us in the direction of infancy and early childhood as a means of comprehending the aetiology of mental disturbance.

But Winnicott championed not only infants and their parents, but also children, adolescents, and adults as well. He really helped to create the professions of child psychiatry and child psychotherapy in Great Britain, and he introduced the fruits of child psychoanalysis into the public sector, serving arguably as the very prototype of the contemporary British National Health Service child psychotherapist, processing, interviewing, and treating large numbers of cases (Kahr, 1996b). He also became one of the first individuals within the psychoanalytical profession to create a multidisciplinary team. Winnicott distinguished himself, of course, not only as a practitioner of intensive, long-term, full psychoanalytical treatment of children, but also as a craftsman of briefer, shorter, consultative work for those boys and girls who neither needed extensive analysis nor craved it; and he explored the possibilities of what he called "on demand" treatment for those children who did not require fixed sessions but, rather, needed to be seen only from time to time (e.g. Winnicott, 1971b, 1978).

Even more, Dr Winnicott became one of the founders of modern family therapy in England by working not only with child patients but also with their parents (Winnicott, 1956, 1960a). He knew so well that mothers and fathers could transmit their psychopathology to their offspring, and that such anxieties must ultimately come to be contained. In a hitherto unpublished letter written to a colleague, K. R. Llewellin, Winnicott observed that

> I used to call my clinic at the Paddington Green Children's Hospital, when I was inclined to give it a nickname, a clinic for the management of maternal or paternal hypochondria. In the simplest cases, and they were very common, my job was to make an examination and to say: "At this moment your child is healthy as far as one can tell. Come again when you are worried." [Winnicott, 1966b]

Winnicott worked with parents, and he also enlisted the assistance of parents as auxiliary therapists, realizing that much of the containment and interpretation of childhood mental illness could be undertaken by mothers or fathers themselves (e.g. Winnicott, 1956, 1960a).

Also, Winnicott theorized extensively about the role of management and residential care in the treatment of the disturbed child, recognizing full well that many disorientated boys and girls required something more than 50-minute psychoanalytical sessions. Occasionally, hospitalization would be required, or at least confinement in a therapeutically orientated care home wherein a greater level of coverage could be provided (e.g. Winnicott, 1943a, 1945c, 1948; cf. Dockar-Drysdale, 1974). His future wife, Clare Britton, assisted him mightily in this clinical observational research on the importance of management (Winnicott & Britton, 1944, 1947). Together, they laid the foundation stones for the field that has come to be known as "forensic child psychotherapy"—the treatment of criminal children and adolescents (e.g. Vizard, Monck, and Misch, 1995; Vizard, Wynick, Hawkes, Woods, & Jenkins, 1996; cf. Kahr, 1996b, in press).

To summarize Winnicott's unparalleled contributions to the study and treatment of infancy and childhood, we can enumerate his legacy thus, in brief phrases:

1. theory of infant psychology;
2. treatment of infant psychopathology;
3. study of infant observation;
4. theory of maternal psychology and psychopathology;
5. theory of paternal psychology;
6. study of hatred of babies;
7. study of foetal psychology;
8. study of perinatal psychology;
9. study of birth trauma;
10. creation of public sector child psychotherapy;
11. development of the multi-disciplinary team;
12. creation of brief psychoanalytical consultations;
13. development of "on demand" treatment;
14. development of family therapy;
15. use of parents as auxiliary therapists;
16. study of management and residential care;
17. promotion of forensic child psychotherapy.

To provide a thorough review of Winnicott's contributions to the field of adult mental health would require an entire separate volume. I shall mention only certain exceptional highlights. Not only did Winnicott bequeath to us an entire theory of human development, tracing the ways in which we progress from the absolute dependence of early infancy to the more independent modes of adult living, but he forged a rich theory of psychoanalytical technique as well, explaining how the phases of treatment mirror those of early development. He also sketched a theory of psychopathology, elucidating various developmental pathways for delinquency, depression, and schizophrenia (Winnicott, 1961, 1963c), and he provided trenchant critiques of sadistic treatments in somatic psychiatry (Winnicott, 1943b, 1944b, 1944c, 1949a).

Winnicott explored the often terrifying world of regression within the clinical situation, and he bravely undertook analytical treatments of some of the most disturbed psychiatric patients, who occasionally lived with him in his home (cf. Kahr, 1996a). He also experimented with the boundaries of classical technique in order to ascertain which parameters would need to be introduced in order to heal the psychotic patient.

Along the way, he introduced an unusually robust selection of new terminology into the mental health literature, notably "transitional object", "transitional phenomena", "holding environment", "facilitating environment", "good-enough mother", "primary maternal preoccupation", "antisocial tendency", "capacity to be alone", "capacity for concern", "absolute dependence", "relative dependence", "towards independence", "hate in the countertransference", "playing", "the use of an object", and others too numerous to mention (cf. Abram, 1996).

As an educationalist, Winnicott performed heroic feats to introduce psychological ideas to colleagues in various allied professions, such as paediatrics, social work, midwifery, and child care. Above all, he attempted to reach parents through his legendary radio broadcasts. Winnicott's extraordinarily lucid and non-persecutory approach to the enlightenment of parents remains a model for all contemporary mental health practitioners (e.g. Winnicott, 1945a).

No one but Donald Winnicott possessed sufficient internal benignity to find the value in depression (Winnicott, 1964a) or to realize that delinquency could be understood as a sign of health (Winnicott, 1968b). Winnicott's achievements can only be described as enormous, encompassing a wide range of fields within child care, paediatrics, psychology, and psychotherapy. Though the importance of Winnicott's work may be self-evident to contemporary professionals and scholars, I suspect that we will not even begin to appreciate the full import of his labours until several further decades will have passed.

The Winnicott Festschrift

I have divided this memorial volume, *The Legacy of Winnicott: Essays on Infant and Child Mental Health*, into four principal sections, each paying tribute to a different aspect of Winnicott's work. In the first part, "Overtures to Winnicott", two distinguished authors provide us with a preliminary glimpse into Winnicott and his world. Dr Robert Langs, one of the most erudite scholars on psychoanalytical technique, assesses Winnicott's place in the history of psychoanalysis, concentrating on Winnicott's sensitivity to the importance of the clinical setting and on the vital role of the interaction between the patient and the psychoanalyst. And Professor Paul Roazen, the distinguished biographer and historian, has very generously permitted me to publish the text of his interview with Donald Winnicott, which he conducted at Winnicott's Belgravia home in 1965. Roazen has furnished us with a document of great historical importance, which permits us the opportunity to enjoy a privileged glance into Winnicott's more private and spontaneous reflections and thoughts.

In the second section of the book, entitled "Mothers and Infants", three eminent psychoanalytical thinkers pay tribute to Winnicott's path-breaking observations about babies and their parents. Mr Lloyd deMause, the leading exponent of modern psychohistory and one of the first psychoanalytical scholars to investigate the psychology of the foetus, provides us with a richly referenced survey of the recent literature on pre-natal psychology—an area of study that proved of great interest to Winnicott, though in the absence of modern technology he himself could only speculate about its precise nature. Dr Stella Acquarone, director of the Parent Infant Clinic in London, has treated perhaps more infants psychotherapeutically than any other clinician since Dr Donald Winnicott. In her paper, Dr Acquarone has identified 11 types of psychoanalytical treatment strategies, which I regard as a highly original contribution to the growing literature on infant mental health. The last paper in this section, written by Dr Judith Trowell, the noted child psychiatrist, psychoanalyst, and child protection specialist, contains an account of Trowell's highly pioneering efforts to introduce Winnicott's infant observational work to such diverse professional groups as physicians and the police force.

The third section, devoted to "Children and Adolescents", contains four pieces by experienced clinicians who practise in a Winnicottian style. Dr Juliet Hopkins, one of Donald Winnicott's last supervisees, describes a rather touching case about a little boy who could not play. Mrs Sira Dermen, a British psychoanalyst and child psychotherapist of Armenian extraction, chronicles her courageous work with some of the child survivors of the devastating Armenian earthquake of 1988. Dermen's work provides a splendid modern illustration of Winnicott's concept of the psychoanalytically informed brief consultation. Dr Alasdair Honeyman, the only paediatrician contributing to this volume of essays, reflects most sensitively on the psychological requirements of contemporary paediatric work. The section concludes with an essay by Professor Susie Orbach, arguably the first British psychotherapist to provide us with a sophisticated psychoanalytical theory of the body and of body image, who extends her original and influential work by elaborating upon the concept of the "false body", exploring important theoretical links with Winnicott's notion of the "false self".

In the fourth and final section, "Reminiscences of Winnicott", Professor E. James Anthony, Mr Hugh Gee, and Mr David Holbrook have each furnished us with revealing thumbnail portraits of certain aspects of Winnicott's character. These sketches help us to obtain a much richer picture of Donald Woods Winnicott as a personality, and I extend my appreciation to these three writers for their enlightening personal memories and reflections. I have also appended a series of previously unpublished documents that will be of interest to Winnicott scholars and to Winnicott enthusiasts.

In 1967, Winnicott visited a psychiatric hospital ward outside London to offer consultation to the staff about the management and treatment of their challenging psychotic patients. On 20 July 1967, the young psychiatrist in charge of the schizophrenic patients, whom I shall not name for reasons of confidentiality, wrote to offer his appreciation to Winnicott: "I cannot close without thanking you for your interest and telling you how much your visit was enjoyed by the nurses and the boys. As one boy said to me afterwards, 'he needs to come again', to which I replied 'you felt he was a great help to you' and the boy said 'a great help to us, but he can be a great help to you, too'."

I can think of no better way to end my tribute to Donald Winnicott, cartographer of infancy and pioneer mental health practitioner, than by having quoted these sage words of a psychotic boy. Winnicott proved a boon not only to his many patients, but to all of us who work with patients as well.

PART ONE

OVERTURES TO WINNICOTT

CHAPTER ONE

D. W. Winnicott:
the transitional thinker

Robert Langs

I begin this chapter by confessing that I have a mind far more inclined to unremembering and repression than would be my preference, if I had a choice. But that inclination helps to explain why I remember only one speaker of the many who graced my analytic institute's Saturday morning guest speaker programme for its fledgling candidates. On the other hand, this tendency of mine to repress makes it uncanny and intriguing that the speaker in question was, as I later rediscovered, none other than Donald Winnicott, the man whom we honour with this volume.

My recall is thin, but I do know that it was a bright, sunny day in the 1960s, and the setting was an old, dingy classroom at King's County Hospital in Brooklyn, New York. Fixed in my mind is a tallish, wiry man with a charming British accent, speaking with great yet reserved animation, chalk in hand, making odd little scribbling diagrams on the portable blackboard that stood beside him. That is the all of it.

The question that I have asked myself many times is this: Why has that particular memory, that man, stayed fixed in my mind all these many years? I have no recollection whatsoever of what he said. And I am certain that much of it was quite unfamiliar to me and out of keeping with the thrust of what I was learning in my classically orientated psychoanalytic institute. Indeed, I am sure that there was no introductory reading of his work and no follow-up discussion of his ideas. It was as if an apparition had material-ized and had come and gone without leaving a trace.

It was many years later that it dawned on me that this man whose image was so set in my mind was Donald Winnicott, and that I had had the privilege of hearing him speak on squiggles and other matters that Saturday morning. For me at the time it was—as so often happens to psychoanalysts because of their overly trained, narrowed range of vision—a lost opportunity.

My mind was totally unprepared for the Winnicott experience. My entire way of thinking about the human mind and the psycho-therapeutic interaction had to change radically in order to appreci-ate the brilliance and creativity of the man. Fortunately for me, I was able to make the necessary changes in the years that followed his visit, so I could receive and find illumination through his work and ideas, as witnessed by the very chapter that you are now reading, which I very much hope reflects my deep appreciation for Winnicott's original and evocative writings.

The question, as I said, is this: Why did the image of a psycho-analyst of whom I knew virtually nothing and whose presentation I did not retain stay with me as it did? The answer lies, I believe, in a unique quality that Donald Winnicott possessed as part of every-thing he did, as a thinker, writer, speaker, and no doubt as a psychotherapist and psychoanalyst as well. Winnicott had the abil-ity to transport his listeners from the world of the familiar and the known to that of the unfamiliar and the unknown. I believe that it was this unusual and marvellous experience of transport that left its indelible mark on my mind, even in the absence of the contents of what he said.

This transforming experience is a prime example of a trait in Winnicott that leads me to describe him as a *transitional thinker*. In doing so, I mean to imply that he was a man whose ideas and pronouncements consistently evoked and continue to evoke (wit-ness this volume) new lines of thought and new ways of thinking in his audiences. Repeatedly and quite naturally, Winnicott ex-pressed himself in ways that originated in accepted dogma and ended up in a very different and unexpected place. It was his evident gift to be the kind of thinker who again and again, were you to listen to and appreciate what he was conveying, shook you out of your complacency and your all too constricted view of the human psyche and brought you into places where your mind had not previously visited—places you never even knew existed.

Properly attended to, reading Winnicott's work and pondering his extraordinary ideas was, and is, certain to bring you into that transitional world between reality and fantasy, truth and illusion, the known and the unknown—a space where the familiar is unfamiliar, given its new context, and the unfamiliar seems to have been with you all along. The space into which Winnicott brings us is not only uncharted, it is inherently inventive, imaginative, and mind-expanding.

In a somewhat more esoteric way, Wilfred Bion was another of these transitional thinkers. As is true of Winnicott, you have only to read Bion to be compelled to shed your established ways of thinking and to open yourself to new modes of thought and conceptualization. Another feature that they both share as writers is that their ideas inherently possess a wide and unusual penumbra of meanings. Their concepts were and are incredibly evocative and capable of taking you into many different directions, some of them quite dizzying. The impact of their work stays with you and keeps you thinking about what you have read for weeks at a time. In their most influential form, the transitional ideas of Donald Winnicott can change your view of yourself and your patients forever.

I cannot help but ask rhetorically: Is it not strange that the two most gifted transitional thinkers I have experienced both had distinct Kleinian leanings? This does not necessarily bear testimony to the validity of the ideas involved, although it would be difficult to fault evocative concepts even when ultimately they prove to be in error. But it does say something, I think, about the freedom of Kleinian thinking compared to the orthodox Freudian approach, and the way in which the Kleinian mode either attracts imaginative thinkers or brings out the imagination of creative thinkers—or both.

So, here was this man set in my mind, someone fascinating whom I had heard speak and whom I had, of necessity, eradicated from my mind in order to finish my analytic training. After all, at the time I heard Winnicott's talk, I was being fashioned into a psychoanalytic interpreting machine who created a setting that faded into the background of an analysis and simply safeguarded a patient's transferences—actually, as I now realize, his or her conscious fantasies about me. My role as an analyst was being strictly delimited, and the setting played a minimal role in this definition.

This seemingly protective set of ground rules was said to allow the patient's so-called transferences to emerge as if they unfolded independently and without interactive influence from the analyst seeking their own absolute realization. Under these vaguely defined conditions, the "transference" could then be traced to its purported genetic roots and interpreted to resolve that ever-present, ever-elusive "transference neurosis" my patients were said to have developed. The world I was being trained to negotiate was one of unconscious fantasies and distortions, of transferences and countertransferences, a world of meaning only in which the relationship and setting were background features that served the interpretative process and little else.

While I have no recollection of it, I feel quite certain now that I must have experienced Winnicott as an aberration—a charming Englishman whose ideas, if I grasped any part of them at the time, must have made absolutely no sense to me as I had no context and receptors with which to receive them. To this day, I wonder why my psychoanalytic institute had invited him to speak to its candidates. His work was not included in its teaching programme, and his very spirit and openness ran counter to the accepted classical dogmas—as it does to this day, though perhaps a bit less so than thirty years ago.

I resurrected this forgotten man soon after I had graduated from my Institute and gained the freedom to explore and to think for myself—though only up to a point, as I soon discovered. In 1968, I was given as a gift the marvellous book by Michael Balint (1968) on *The Basic Fault: Therapeutic Aspects of Regression.* Oddly enough, while ultimately analysts must learn primarily from their patients, highly original books always have been a major impetus for my own forays into the unknown and in the development of my thinking. Balint's book was the first of several such influential volumes—it was the right book at the right time.

Balint's work, some of it borrowed from Winnicott, helped to initiate my personal transition from a well-trained and highly disciplined classical psychoanalyst to an adaptational–interactional–communicative psychoanalyst with a very different purview. I can still picture the references to Winnicott's work in that book, and at the centre of it all, for me at least, were the concepts of the facilitating environment and the holding environment, perhaps Winnicott's most important contributions to the technique and theory of the therapeutic process.

The conceptualization of the many ramifications of the analyst's management of the setting—the ground rules and frame of psychotherapy—was absolutely astounding to me at the time. The metaphors each writer used fired my imagination and thinking. Balint wrote of the analyst's creating an unobtrusive medium for the communications and experiences of the patient, much like the water that allows a swimmer to swim. And Winnicott wrote of the holding environment, the way that the analyst safely holds the patient as a mother holds a child.

It was for me much like hearing a new language or entering a strange new world of unforeseen experience and power. As a writer and psychotherapist, I would never again be the same. Winnicott's writings, which I quickly pursued and read avidly, catalysed a lasting transition for which I am forever grateful. If there is indeed any creativity in my own, a major impetus and contribution came from the pages of Winnicott's (1958a, 1965) major volumes of professional writings, which are remarkable in their originality and wisdom. The holding environment concept came to me at a time when I was working within the framework of the classical principles related to the ground rules—that the analyst establishes a set of conditions for the analysis, such as fixing the time for the sessions, charging a fee, maintaining privacy and relative anonymity, and such, and then manages this frame when issues arise with flexibility and little thought as to their impact on the patient or the analysis. As I indicated, these very technical and mechanical measures were said to be needed to safeguard the transference, and once established, they created a setting that receded into the background of the analysis, while interpreting the so-called transference made up the foreground.

Now here was Winnicott telling me, directly and by implication, that the analyst's management of the setting is a way of holding and even healing the patient—that the setting is a dynamic force, and its management is a way of caring for the patient in a therapeutic sense, and also of interacting with that patient, a means by which the analyst intervenes in ways other than making interpretations, efforts that strongly influence the patient both consciously and unconsciously, and which may well be fateful to the outcome of the analysis.

The difference between these two worlds was monumental and far-reaching for me in countless ways. My images and understanding of the therapeutic experience and situation, of the patient and the psychotherapist, and the process of cure were all changed and broadened forever. The holding environment idea led me to the literature on the ground rules of psychoanalysis, and to clinical observations of the effects of managing the framework of treatment. It was a new world filled with unforeseen, telling revelations.

The need to understand in depth the nature, effects, and techniques related to the ground rules of psychotherapy brought me directly to the immediate therapeutic interaction. It was one of the major motives that prompted me to investigate communication in psychotherapy and psychoanalysis and to detail the specifics of the spiralling, mutually interactive and adaptive conscious and unconscious communications between patients and therapists. This proved to be the beginning of my own approach to understanding the psychotherapy interaction and the realm of emotionally charged communication and experiences—and the related adaptations and maladaptations. It is an exploration with as yet, some twenty years later, no end in sight.

All in all, Winnicott's work has helped to transform me from a non-writer to the author of some 125 papers and 34 books. Although you may want to frown a bit at the transitional powers of Winnicott's writings in light of this effusiveness on my part, I am more inclined to thank him for shaking me out of my rigidities and blindnesses and for opening up a world of discovery for me.

This discussion brings me to one of my favourites among the countless evocative, transitional quotes from Winnicott, all of which have spawned a wide range of responsive ideas and fresh perspectives in my mind. I refer to his notion that analysts write papers and books as a way of completing their own personal analysis. I have, unsurprisingly, often pondered what there could have been about my own analysis that has made it necessary for me to carry out such an excess of self-healing investigations and writings. I also wonder what my analyst thinks about all of this—whether or not he has read Winnicott. What could this need be about?

In trying to answer this question, I am brought to two unexpected, but mind-opening, considerations. The first touches on the always knotty problem of so-called training analyses. Are they ever complete in any satisfying "enough things were insightfully and holding-wise resolved" way? Or are they always in need of finishing, writers trying to effect that final resolution one way, non-writers doing it via other means—not a few of them by turning to a second analysis, and many others doing so in inappropriate ways through their work with their patients?

There are two critical factors that convince me that every training analysis is in some significant way unfinished. The first lies with how psychoanalysts conduct their analyses, which raises many questions that I cannot develop here except to note the likelihood of much in the way of unanalysed issues and unrecognized countertransference-based inputs—passed onto them by their own training analyst—that inevitably leave analysands with residuals that they must work out for themselves (cf. Langs, 1992a, 1992b, 1993a, 1993b, 1995).

The second factor is related to the first, and here even Winnicott must be called into question. It pertains to how psychoanalysts manage the setting with their analysands. It was Winnicott's genius to recognize the importance and impact of the analyst's management of the ground rules and setting of an analysis, yet his own handling of the frame, which was quite loose, would raise many problems in terms of the likely unconscious detrimental influence that his management efforts had on his patients. But here Winnicott is representative of most training analysts who create loosely managed and easily modified frames for their analyses of candidates, and as a result, as shown through studies of the unconscious effects of lax frame management on patients (Langs, 1992a, 1993a, 1993b, 1995), leave their terminated patients with unanalysed difficulties, many of them iatrogenic in nature.

All of this is implicit in Winnicott's comment about the analysand's need to complete his or her own analysis through some self-healing means. But there is, as well, another more serious and broader problem implicitly addressed through this insight—a prime example of the different directions in which a single Winnicott remark can take you. There are grave reasons to object to the claims made by many psychotherapists that a particular patient's creative output during and after therapy was a result and confirmation of a sound and healing therapeutic effort. Often these claims fly in the face of everything we have come to accept about sound forms of treatment. These psychotherapists violate their patients' inviolable need for and right to a strong holding approach with an optimal setting and well-secured ground rules and a basically interpretative effort with encoded validations from the patient. This touches on our enormous uncertainty as to the effects of psychotherapists' interventions in the short- and long term, our problems in identifying sound treatment practices, and our confusion regarding the nature of psychotherapeutic cure—a most disturbing set of issues regarding which little clarity has emerged.

I am reminded of the poet Anne Sexton, whose tape-recorded sessions by one therapist and open sexual seduction by another are well known (Middlebrook, 1991). Despite the fact that she ended her life in suicide, these therapists claim that their efforts made their patient into a gifted poet—this said in the most positive sense, as if it came from sound interventions and confirmed the validity and value of their techniques, blatant frame deviations and all. But here is Winnicott warning us that creativity in psychoanalysts/patients comes at least in part from what has remained unresolved in their analysis. This could correctly imply that erroneous and harmful interventions are the basis for much of the creativity in many patients, rather than the proposed therapeutic unleashing of creative energies. That is, inventiveness in patients may well derive more from a psychotherapist's errors and harm than from the psychotherapist's sound work.

One of the great assets of the evolved human mind, easily misused and abused by psychotherapists, lies in its power to mobilize enormous resources in the face of trauma and adversity—damage from psychotherapists included. Just as we all must heal the psychological wounds imposed on us, however unwittingly, by our parents, so there is little doubt that we are left with a similar task after time spent with our analysts or psychotherapists. The complexity of the psychotherapeutic experience and the human condition precludes an unmarred treatment journey. For greater or lesser reasons, being in and ending a psychotherapy means having to resolve residual pieces of dysfunction. The hope is to do this work creatively instead of poorly or not at all.

Another favourite strand in Winnicott's work takes me into a rather different set of realizations. Winnicott wrote that he interpreted to patients to let them know where his ignorance began. With these words, I am off on another transition. It begins with the classical mode of thinking where an interpretation imparts therapist knowledge, if not brilliance, and is correct until proven to be in error. And it bridges from there into another world, where the interventions of the psychotherapist communicate far more than his or her understanding and have a wide range of effects well beyond the consciously intended and recognized meanings—whether or not the therapist is aware of them.

This Winnicott pronouncement again helped to free me from a conceptual straitjacket in which the focus in intervening lies entirely with the consciously intended meanings of an interpretation. His concept gives us the freedom—even demands that we take it—to explore the many messages embodied in an interpretation other than the narrow interpretative focus on which most of us have been trained to focus, and beyond which we may not see.

Every interpretation carries with it an enormous number of consciously implied and unconsciously conveyed implications that exist well beyond the psychotherapist's intended cognitive statement. Each embodies, as Winnicott noted, the revelation of one's limits of understanding, but each may also convey a variety of biases and blind spots, the state of the psychotherapist's holding capacities, his or her attitudes towards the facilitating environment and the ground rules of therapy, and an infinite number of conscious and unconscious meanings generated and imparted by the psychotherapist idiosyncratically in response to the patient's material, but far from what the patient intended to express—all this and far more.

In a single pronouncement that turns our usual thinking on its head, Winnicott gives us food for endless thought. But this is what this marvellous transitional thinker offers again and again as an endowment to those of us who are more conservative and single-minded in our thinking. There is good reason too for each of us who are relatively set in our ways of thinking—and how rare the exceptions are—to adopt Winnicott as our model. Think differently once a day, he is telling us, embrace ideas that transcend your fixed position and allow these ideas to take you into unexplored territories—after all, you can, if need be, return to more familiar ground long before you see your next patient.

One of the most unfortunate attributes of psychoanalysis is that we are virtually all practitioners offering services to our patients. We need a solid core of stable ideas and precepts with which to work, and so do our patients. This means that expanding our thinking comes with unwelcome uncertainty and difficulty. We are imprisoned by our need for certitude—which we never quite achieve anyhow.

Paradoxically, we need to train ourselves to surrender our training, if only for an hour or two whenever we can. Thinking transitionally is truly a mind-expanding experience, as Winnicott has shown us. From time to time, we should pause to read him and to follow him down that inherently creative, transforming pathway that he cleared for us. We will certainly be the wiser for doing so.

CHAPTER TWO

A meeting with Donald Winnicott in 1965

Paul Roazen

very interview that I conducted with any of the early psychoanalysts always succeeded in teaching me something
special. While many of those that I saw during my most
intense fieldwork during the mid-1960s were either relatively
obscure then or have been generally forgotten by now, Donald
Winnicott remains an outstanding exception to any such generali-
zation. For, rather to my amazement, his stature has continued to
grow, so that there is now not only a large bust of him at the
headquarters of the British Psycho-Analytical Society, but his writings have been translated into many languages. With the passage
of time, his reputation has eclipsed that of many who were once
considered leading representatives of the profession.

It is true that at the time I proposed to see Winnicott in September of 1965, he had already been recommended to me by someone
as reliably intellectual as Dr Charles Rycroft as "the genius of
British analysis". Rycroft went through Winnicott's (1958a) book
Collected Papers: Through Paediatrics to Psycho-Analysis in order to
help tutor me about which articles I ought to read first.

At the outset of my contact with Winnicott, he indicated that he
had heard about me from Masud Khan, and that I was reportedly

"an assiduous reader". Khan was then in charge of Ernest Jones's papers at the British Psycho-Analytical Society, and he had given me the green light to inspect the material there, even though Khan himself underestimated the significance of what I could find in Jones's raw files. I gathered that Khan, who kept a picture of Winnicott in his apartment, was on close personal terms with Winnicott. I had heard that Khan helped Winnicott with compiling the index to more than one of his books, and I supposed that he did other editorial chores for Winnicott as well. But I admit that it never dawned on me that Khan might still then be in analysis with Winnicott, although that now turns out to have been the case. At the time Khan seemed already so senior a figure within psychoanalysis that the thought that he might have been a patient of Winnicott's never crossed my mind. As far as I can tell, Khan, a vocal Francophile with many important friends in Paris, was personally responsible for helping to introduce Winnicott in France. There was also some correspondence between Winnicott and Jacques Lacan. In Khan's (1988) controversial book, *When Spring Comes: Awakenings in Clinical Psychoanalysis*, we find a plausible-sounding account of how Winnicott behaved clinically with patients.

My own response to Winnicott was that he seemed very much like a pixie: he was full of an extraordinary kind of whimsical, childlike charm, and I found him disarming and wonderful to spend time with. Yet he also had a rather weak grasp of theory and of the history of psychoanalytic concepts, which is where I assumed Khan could help him. Winnicott was strikingly unlike someone as original as Erich Fromm, who had what I considered a Germanic concern for systematization. While Fromm's standing in psychoanalysis is now relatively marginal (although probably no analyst's writings are as accessible to airport bookstore browsers), Winnicott still seems to be gaining in ascendancy. A book of his letters has come out (Winnicott, 1987), his papers are widely studied, and the literature about him continues to grow (Kahr, 1996a).

The examples of both Winnicott and Fromm should prove that it is possible to go beyond Freud, using his methods to reach conclusions that he might have found abhorrent. Such writers deserve, I think, to be considered an important part of the thinking of psychoanalysis as a whole. Freud did develop his ideas out of his own autobiographical understanding, and therefore all the historical fascination with his life, which shows no sign of abating, is fully justified. But in the end it is possible to emerge from his work with a variety of different points of view without being guilty of some treason to his basic cause.

I saw Winnicott only that once in London. We spent an afternoon together in his consulting-room, where he also served me an impromptu meal. When he reported what he had heard about myself as a reader, he was admitting that it was not true of himself. I suspect now that he was a good deal more cultured than he was inclined to let on.

He had started off as a paediatrician before specializing in the psychoanalytic treatment of children, and he used to work with them by means of their drawings (which he called "squiggles"). Almost at the start of our time together he handed me a marvellous sketchbook to use as a writing pad to support my note-taking. He claimed to have originally been an inhibited Englishman, with few outlets in fantasy except for music. I found him a wonderfully free and open person.

He mentioned how similar to Freud's impact on him that of Charles Darwin had once been—both had revealed a new world to him. "What a release it was!" he told me. He had been surprised to discover, when he got to Cambridge as an undergraduate, that there were such beings as Darwinians. He himself had come from a religious background, as had a number of other early British analysts. He had come across a book by Oskar Pfister, an early analyst who was also a Swiss pastor, and this had helped him initially to read through Freud.

Winnicott said that he had had "a disturbed adolescence". He had been "very normal" until he was nine years old, and then suddenly he could not remember his dreams any more. Being cut off from his dreaming was disturbing to him. Later, he therefore asked a librarian what she could recommend on dreams. She gave him a book by the French philosopher Henri Bergson, which was "no help", and then another text, until finally he came to Freud's (1900a) *The Interpretation of Dreams*. Subsequently, Winnicott happened to have a medical student friend who was already personally in analysis, and Winnicott decided that this was for him too.

Winnicott went to see Ernest Jones, who gave him a list of names of possible psychoanalysts; but this was of "no use" since

Winnicott did not know what to do with these references. Jones had proceeded to "reel off" not only the symptoms of which Winnicott was already aware, but also those that were to come up during his analyses later. Jones had been "absolutely right", and Winnicott considered him quite a "show-off".

Winnicott chose to go to James Strachey for an analysis that lasted almost ten years. Strachey was about as bookish as it is possible to be, and I find it hard to imagine what kind of therapist he could ever have been. He seemed at a special sort of distance from usual human contact. The correspondence between James Strachey and his wife Alix Strachey (1924) implies an absence in Winnicott of a sexual interest in the wife he continued to be married to for years; a lack of normal masculinity in Winnicott might unfortunately fit in with his fascination with children. Because of his clinical work with youngsters, Winnicott became interested in the ideas that Melanie Klein had begun to develop. Strachey was by no means anti-Klein, but he said that he could not teach Klein to Winnicott in analysis, so Winnicott went to her directly to learn about play therapy by bringing her a case of his. He got on well with her and finally finished his analysis with her disciple Joan Riviere. Both Winnicott's analysts were non-medical and had been analysed in Vienna by Freud.

As far as Winnicott was concerned, Freud's technique was ideally suited for the psychoneurotics, which "one sees so rarely nowadays", largely due to the fact that people can read for themselves widely circulated texts "like the Pelican editions of Freud's works". Clinically, Winnicott said that he saw so-called borderline cases all the time, like those in Breuer and Freud's (1895d) *Studies on Hysteria*. The term "borderline" seems to me to have become as much a waste-basket category as the concept "neurosis" once was.

I think that what first charmed me about Winnicott was his early emphasis in our talk on "the danger of sanity in psychoanalysis". He proposed that the "flight to sanity" was "quite a problem", which I found in refreshing contrast to the dull-as-dishwater conception of normality that one tended to get in North American ego-psychological thinking. As Winnicott (1945b, p. 140, fn. 3) himself once wrote, "we are poor indeed if we are only sane". According to Kleinian theory, psychosis is closer to health than one might guess; paradoxically, neurosis is less apt to be self-healing. This whole line of thinking implies that symptoms can sometimes be both constructive and self-healing—a view that the British psychiatrist Ronald Laing would make widely popular in the 1960s (cf. Laing, 1960).

Edward Glover, who had once been Jones's second-in-command, gave me many hours of his time in 1965 and 1966. Glover is, I believe, one of those analysts who have had a raw deal in being relatively forgotten or at least are undervalued now. The most orthodox Kleinians even blamed Glover for the split between Klein and her daughter Melitta Schmideberg. Like Winnicott, Glover had said to me that there is much sanity that has a symptomatic quality. Winnicott thought it "a pity" that Glover left the British Psycho-Analytical Society, which he would himself head twice as president, since Glover had such a "good head". Masud Khan told me how ineffective he had been in trying to lure Glover back into teaching British analysts. Erich Fromm, too, was critical of normality as part of his distrust of conformism. But Fromm never mentioned Winnicott to me, and I doubt that Winnicott had ever read much Fromm.

Winnicott had consciously benefited more from Carl Gustav Jung's ideas than Fromm had. Winnicott (1964b) had even written a long, appreciative review of Jung's autobiography. I asked Winnicott a number of questions, and I shall reproduce these here, italicized, using my exact words.

What kind of reaction did the review provoke? Winnicott mentioned that one of the leading Jungians in London, Dr Michael Fordham, whom I had also met, thought "very well" of it. The review was what Fordham himself "would have liked to have written, except that he was too close to it".

Was the contrast between Freud and Jung that of a man with a self at odds with a man still in search of a self? Winnicott replied, "Yes"—but for Winnicott the question also remained, "Was Freud's self a false one?" The distinction between "true self" and "false self" was one with so many traditional philosophical overtones that I am pretty sure that Freud would have disapproved of it, since he sought to make his psychology scientific in an empirical sense. But for me it echoed the issue of authenticity, raised, for example, by Fromm. Winnicott said that he had once mentioned Jung's name at a meeting of the British Psycho-Analytical Society, but the hush was so striking that he dared not repeat the exercise. Winnicott was proud that the British Psycho-Analytical Society had remained unified and not split, despite all the ideological differences of opinion that had coexisted.

Since I was seeing Winnicott at a time when Freud's work had come under sustained assault from feminist critics, and after both Erich Fromm as well as Karen Horney had earlier made a great deal out of the inadequacies of Freud's conception of femininity, that seemed a logical line of inquiry to pursue.

Did Freud err about female psychology? Winnicott answered that it is certainly true that in Freud "one finds only women who want to be men, never men envying women". In order to get at the more serious disturbances, no matter how normal the patient may appear, the person has to go through a psychosis in the analytic consulting-room. This proposition, which many other analysts as well as non-analysts would consider highly dubious, followed from Klein's thinking that the infant displays psychotic tendencies and that it is therapeutic for patients seriously to regress. Freud himself "could not accept" the maternal in himself because he was so strong a paternal head of his family. But, as Winnicott remarked, "Yet the maternal is inextricably linked to the infantile". And therefore Winnicott thought he could explain why Freud would have been personally blocked from adopting a less rationalistic approach to therapy. Freud could tolerate and indeed was "attracted by" his feminine side, as long as it was located outside, in Sándor Ferenczi or in other followers like him.

What about Freud's addiction to smoking? How would it affect his clinical practice? Winnicott viewed Freud's smoking not just as a question of nicotine, but as something that hinged on the psychology of his being able to put something into his mouth. The issue is not just the presence of repressed homosexuality, although it is that, "of course". But on a deeper level he regarded the smoking as being related to an attempt by Freud to "recapture and make up for the loss of the experience of omnipotence". Some people never have that experience. But the smoking can be seen to present a form of "control over the mother". She becomes incorporated yet not swallowed, and then the loss is made up.

What about Freud's fainting fits with Jung? It means, Winnicott supposed, "a feminine identification". It is characteristically Jewish, after all, not to be able to tolerate "an iota of femininity" in oneself or in one's eldest son. Freud's difficulties here help to explain why he remained at bottom "blind to pre-oedipal" problems. Freud wanted to leave the mother and the feminine out, and he reserved it all to nursemaids and such. But in spite of these striking defects in his thinking, Winnicott thought that "Freud's supreme achievement was the development of his technique".

Were Jones's own analytic contributions rather slight? Winnicott believed that Jones was "not terribly original". Certainly he had proceeded to apply Freud's "discoveries" all over the place. Jones's (1916) article on symbolism was important (and Glover had thought so too), as is Jones's (1927) notion that annihilation anxiety has to be considered deeper than neurosis—psychotic, in fact. In those early days, the fear that obsessed everybody was the castration anxiety that Freud thought so central to neurosis.

Although Winnicott had not trained in psychiatry, he was notable for being more open to the significance of psychosis than the traditional Freudians; it was related, I think, to Winnicott's special interest in the psychology of children.

A dream may be structurally like a psychosis, as Freud thought, but does it not function very differently? Patients who have psychotic experiences often say that it is exactly as if they were having a dream. The big trouble, though, is that they are awake—in a sense, they cannot fall properly asleep. Winnicott commented that, "It makes all the difference in the world."

Would Freud have failed to recognize the positive, ego-integrative functions of the dream? Winnicott saw dreams in terms of release, which is different from fulfilment. The idea of the constructive uses of regression comes much later in psychoanalytic theory. In reality, Jung had developed this concept first, although it was better developed later among orthodox Freudians by Ernst Kris. When Freud describes a dream as being like a psychosis, nobody would say that nowadays. A certain kind of dream does not even need to be analysed "at all"; it just means that the analysis has got so far. Winnicott had those kinds of dreams after he was out of analysis. It is terribly important to be in contact with one's dream life and to be able to talk about it to one's analyst. The specific interpretation that is offered "really matters much less". At this point, I could better understand how Winnicott had lain on Strachey's couch for so many years; Winnicott was so full of his own ideas as probably to have been relatively impervious to an uncomprehending analyst.

Winnicott tried to arrange his consulting-room carefully for his patients. They could get in "a tremendous row" with him some-times over the arrangement of the room. The setting is an entirely non-verbal aspect of the situation, yet it acts like an interpretation, even though the analyst has been completely silent. "The impor-tant thing is that the analyst does not die, and that he does not retaliate", no matter what happens in the patient's life or what he says. The analyst's job can sometimes be just to sit there and be a "bad" analyst for the patient.

Being "a bad analyst" was what Winnicott thought Wilhelm Fliess had been for Freud. (It seems to me unfortunate that Winni-cott, Glover, and other analysts understood Freud's friendship with Fliess on the model of the analytic encounter.) Winnicott even thought that perhaps Freud did not "ever read" Fliess's letters. That cannot have been literally true, but I took Winnicott to be saying something important about the inevitable self-involvement of all creative activity. Obviously, Fliess was "an idealization" for Freud, which had to lead to disappointment. No real evidence exists that Fliess had any idea of the "discoveries" that Freud was coming up with.

Winnicott had a love for psychological paradox that I found especially engaging; for example, he maintained that it is easier for a man to analyse the maternal components in his patients "pre-cisely because the analyst does not have breasts". With female patients, there is no danger of homosexual involvements, and with males it means that they will not get stuck at that early stage, for they can "get out of it". Yet the practice of analysis puts "a great strain", Winnicott held, on the male analyst.

Winnicott was struck by the example of how John Rickman had gone to Freud with a particular infantile memory. The memory was of Rickman as a small child lying in his cot with pneumonia and thinking that he was going to die. He saw a round object at both ends of the curtain rod. On one side, the round object started to turn; he knew it was not really turning, and yet it was so for him. Apparently, this was a very disturbing memory, and it was what he took to Freud in his analysis. But Freud was "not able to help him on it at all"—he told Rickman that he was "psychotic" and had "best get out of being an analyst".

When Rickman's mother died, he recounted to Winnicott how he had held her ashes in an urn and turned it about. "Now I have you in my control"—that is what he thought at the grave. Rickman felt that now he could tell her what he really thought of her. Winnicott did not connect the two things, the urn and the infantile memory, until after Rickman's death; Winnicott had wanted to "burst into tears" at the story of the graveside. Rickman always remained "bothered" by the same memory. It hinged, according to Winnicott's interpretation, on Rickman's projection of himself onto his mother's breast in order to keep control of her. Klein was responsible for the symbolic standing of the breast for British analysts. Freud had, however, been unable to do anything with that memory of Rickman's supposed identification with his mother's breast.

Rickman had many good stories about Freud: for instance, that Freud's colleagues used to smuggle cigars into the crates of the psychoanalytic press being shipped to Vienna. Winnicott also shook his head, sadly, about the obsessional notes Rickman had kept on patients, which proved of "no use" to anyone after his death. Rickman had evidently been planning some sort of study of Freud's concepts. In his writing, Rickman "dramatized" things—those examples in his book with Geoffrey Gorer on Russia are not "strictly true" (Gorer & Rickman, 1949). The illustrations were drawn from several individual instances, but they were only "dramatically true".

Winnicott thought that Rickman's early troubling memory was a model for what had needed to be done in changing psychoanalysis as Freud had left it. Like Edoardo Weiss and others, Donald Winnicott thought that the problem of psychosis could not be left in the outer darkness to which Freud had often consigned it. And Winnicott himself had become especially interested in defences against the loss of the experience of omnipotence. Cigar smoking, for example, means that the cigar is not lost: it is incorporated, but not swallowed. Of course, this was a line that Freud himself, with all his own smoking, could not have pursued. But Winnicott was convinced that Freud had done quite enough for one man. His self-analysis went so far, and really quite far enough. As Winnicott opined, "If he had been able to go further, he would not have been capable of making the original contributions."

Winnicott saw himself as someone who was moving psycho-analysis beyond how Freud had left it, and he felt indebted to Melanie Klein's thinking. She had felt that when Anna Freud came over to England, she was menaced; it was to be the end of the "happy, productive" period of British psychoanalysis. Of course, "Mrs Klein was not at all a scientist." But she was "very original and creative". Whether Anna Freud was really such a threat to her or whether that was "a delusion" it is impossible to say. In any case, Klein withdrew and set up her own system with her follow-ers. Glover then—"as people usually do"—proceeded to enter into her dread of enemies. Winnicott noted: "It [had] been such an exciting and prolific period; and then she shrank back, and it was over."

After World War II, Winnicott felt ready to do some lecturing. Yet neither Mrs Klein nor Miss Freud would have him on their different training programmes. Fortunately, he had "other irons in the fire". Mrs Klein proceeded to build up "a closed system". There is even an introduction of Mrs Riviere's to one of Mrs Klein's books where she implies that "there is nothing new to be discovered".

Like other analysts who became unusually creative, Winnicott remembered how taken in by psychoanalytic thinking he had at first been: "What a pest I must have been to my friends around 1926!" His new knowledge of the unconscious led him to insist on pointing out to others that various things in everyday life "meant" such and such. Winnicott was then using Freud "all over the place". He thought that such an excess was really a phase-appro-priate stage. Part of Winnicott's attractiveness later as an analytic theorist was that he did not communicate the spirit of being a know-it-all.

Did he ever meet Freud? No, he did not, although he could have done so in 1938 or 1939, after Freud had emigrated to London. But Freud did not want to see new people, and Winnicott did not desire to be "cruel" about it.

How central a flaw was Freud's outlook on women? Freud thought that they were just like men—except that they are not, and there-fore Freud considered them as "frustrated men". Freud had his own female "anima". That was one of the rare occasions on which I encountered somebody using a specifically Jungian term in order to understand Freud. The feminist critique of Freud was then too fresh for me to have had the necessary distance to see the anachronistic side of some of the charges: not only did women thrive in psychoanalysis as a profession, but in the context of his own times Freud can be seen as a progressive force: for example, he insisted over opposition with the Vienna Psycho-Analytical Society that women be admitted to full membership.

At the time that I saw Winnicott, he had a patient that bore on the issue of male homosexuality that he was trying to write about. The issue that Winnicott wondered about was: what has stopped the patient from engaging in homosexual practices? Winnicott thought that the patient "unconsciously knew" that he was a woman, although he also knew that it was not true; he did not want his unconscious conviction to be disproved. This was an example of Winnicott's playfully topsy-turvy thinking. Male homosexuality, for Winnicott, could not be explained just on the basis of feminine identifications.

Winnicott was already well known enough to have done guest lecturing in the United States, and so I asked his opinions of the people we knew in common. *What did he think of the people he met in Boston, Massachusetts?* He was not very impressed. He had stayed with Elizabeth Zetzel. I knew from Edward Glover that Glover had considered Zetzel as Jones's "pet". Winnicott called her "clever" and "a restless spirit", and he hoped that she might turn out to have "a very original mind". She died prematurely in 1970. He also remembered having met Beata "Tola" Rank, and he "quite liked her" (Roazen, 1990). Winnicott felt responsible for introducing into the British Psycho-Analytical Society in the late 1930s the idea that one "liked" someone, and that Anna Freud had "picked it up" from him. Winnicott thought that Otto Rank had done "good work" after proposing his theory of the birth trauma. By chance, Winnicott and his first wife had been on the Forbes island in Massachusetts. Winnicott knew that Malcolm Forbes had killed himself, but I am not sure that he was aware of how closely linked Rank had been with the Forbes family.

Winnicott claimed that Anna Freud had been very generous in citing him. Yet it seemed "rather ridiculous" that all American students read one article of his, on "transitional objects", because of her having used it in her bibliographies. "Obviously", they had not read anything else by him, since they always cited the article from the *International Journal of Psycho-Analysis* (Winnicott, 1953), where it had appeared originally, and not from his book of collected papers (Winnicott, 1958a).

Winnicott thought that "one cannot get properly analysed in America". The Americans were more orthodoxly Freudian than the British, partly out of their great deference to Anna Freud. But in America, if an analyst tried to meet a patient's needs in a regression during a session, then the analyst would be regarded as naughty or "wild". The best people in America seemed to him preoccupied with maintaining training "standards"; and psychoanalysis did spread "awfully fast" there. But his own experiences as a child analyst made him much less concerned about fulfilling any of the traditional analytic properties; he was unconcerned about whether the patient was on the couch or on the floor. Once upon a time he would have been terribly worried about whether or not he was a proper analyst—a concern expressed by other analysts in talking about having had the same early anxieties.

What did he think about Erikson's ego psychology? Winnicott enviously wished that he were the author of Erik Erikson's books—this was said with the utmost conviction. Winnicott told me that Erikson was the only one in analysis about whom he felt that way. Winnicott himself claimed to be "no good" at theory. When Erikson had been in London once and had seen patients at a children's clinic, he could spot something positive in each of them: "he was not making it up, either". Winnicott, who had recently been asked to review a revised edition of Erikson's (1950) *Childhood and Society*, asked me to send Erikson his best greetings.

Winnicott also thought that Heinz Hartmann was "a giant" with "really tremendous clinical experience". Hartmann's ego psychology was supposedly "a help" in treating psychotics. I already knew about Erikson's tortured relationship to Anna Freud; Winnicott not only talked about Martin James's struggle to disengage himself from "Miss Freud", but was also aware of the inhibitions that Jones worked under while writing his biography of Freud because of her position in London. Like others, Winnicott thought that Ernest Jones had been brave in going to Vienna to rescue the Freuds in 1938 and also courageous in finishing his biography of Freud despite the onset of serious ill health.

What about Paul Federn's ideas on psychosis? Despite Edoardo Weiss's efforts on behalf of keeping Federn's work alive and Erikson's acknowledgement of how important Federn had been to his own development, Winnicott did not know about him at all, even in connection with what Federn had written about the self.[1]

Winnicott did understand that the biased story of Sándor Ferenczi's relation to Freud, as promoted by Jones, needed to be told properly. I gave Winnicott a citation to a case of Freud's that Weiss had told me about: an agoraphobic patient had, under analysis, turned into a schizophrenic, and had then been "cured" by a re-imposition of the agoraphobia through hypnosis. This case fitted with Winnicott thinking that a psychotic condition could emerge from the removal of a neurotic symptom. He was operating on the explicit assumption of a psychological basis for mental disorder; for him, psychosis was a result of early maternal failure. When he rejected Freud's traditional view that psychotics cannot "transfer" in therapy and are therefore inaccessible to treatment, I thought this position was part of Winnicott's psychological optimism. He pooh-poohed the possibility of a biochemical basis for psychosis. Nor did he think much of the power of the hereditary element in schizophrenia. Here other analysts were to be more precise: Sándor Rado, for instance, had notably insisted on the significance of genetics for psychiatry.

When Winnicott got wind of all my own historical interests, he said with conviction: "It is going to be possible to write volumes and volumes on the intellectual history of psychoanalysis." It seemed to me unusual, and extraordinarily nice of Winnicott, that after he had given me so much time—in fact, we spent hours together—he turned before I left and thanked me for the discussion. I had never encountered anyone more gracious, and spontaneously so, in helping me with my research.

---

[1] Winnicott did in fact correspond with Paul Federn in 1949, though he seems to have forgotten this fact in his interview with Paul Roazen (cf. Winnicott, 1949c). [*Ed.*]

PART TWO

MOTHERS AND INFANTS

CHAPTER THREE

The personality of the foetus

Lloyd deMause

> There is much more continuity between intra-uterine life and earliest infancy than the impressive caesura of the act of birth would have us believe.
>
> [Freud, 1926, p. 138]

Donald Winnicott's beginnings as a paediatrician gave him a unique ability to empathize with children and with the childhood experiences of his adult patients. But Winnicott's genius allowed him to take a giant step further: he did not hesitate to acknowledge the reality of foetal experiences—and even the foetal personality—in his patients, to help them relive perinatal trauma and resolve some of their deepest anxieties.

The origins of foetal psychology

Even though Freud (1900a, p. 400) said that he had come to believe that "the act of birth is the first experience of anxiety", Winnicott had no major psychoanalytic writings on foetal memories to draw upon. However, taking pains to separate his observations from Rank's (1924) birth-trauma speculations, Winnicott (1949b) wrote a major paper on the subject: "Birth Memories, Birth Trauma, and Anxiety". This seminal article, however, was little noticed, since, as he said: "It is rare to find doctors who believe that the experience of birth is important to the baby, that it could have any significance in the emotional development of the individual, and that memory traces of the experience could persist and give rise to trouble even in the adult" (Winnicott, 1949b, p. 175).

When still a paediatrician, Winnicott saw first-hand that new-born babies varied enormously and that prolonged labour could be traumatic for the foetus, resulting in extreme anxiety—so much so that he thought "some babies are born paranoid, by which I mean in a state of expecting persecution" (Winnicott, 1988, p. 149).

Winnicott, however, applied his knowledge many times in ana-lysing his patients. With children, he would allow them to work through foetal memories directly:

> This boy, who was then five, spent a month or two of his analysis testing out my ability to accept his approaches. . . . Eventually he came to sit on my lap. . . . He would get inside my coat and turn upside down and slide down to the ground between my legs; this he repeated over and over again. . . . After this experience I was prepared to believe that memory traces of birth can persist. Of course the same thing in play has turned up in many analyses. [Winnicott, 1949b, pp. 177–178]

With adult patients, Winnicott emphasized that, unlike Rank, he believed that

> interpretations will not suddenly produce total and permanent relief. It is rather this, that since the birth trauma is real it is a pity to be blind to it, and in certain cases and at certain points the analysis absolutely needs acceptance of birth material in among all the other material. [Winnicott, 1949b, p. 180]

He would therefore allow patients—particularly those whose false self remained unchanged after several years—to experience deep regressive states on the couch, and he accepted their birth elements as they occurred. One woman, who had had a "classical" analysis for several years but whose illness remained unchanged, had the unusual habit of falling off the couch. He eventually recognized this as a repetition of birth. When he became open to this, his patient relived, a dozen or more times, various elements of the birth process, acting out breathing changes, constrictions of the body, severe pressure on her head, convulsive movements, and fears of annihilation (Winnicott, 1954). Winnicott promised to write a full paper on this patient, but he never did. Recapturing and working through these body memories—something that most other analysts working in the 1940s would certainly have missed— meant a new start for the patient.

Research into foetal memory

Much has changed in our knowledge of the foetus during the four decades since Winnicott made his pioneering excursions into pre-natal psychology and perinatal psychology. Neurobiologists have made startling advances in the understanding of how the brain develops in the womb, experimental psychologists have discov-ered a great deal about foetal learning, paediatricians have linked all kinds of later problems to foetal distress, and one psychoanalyst has even begun to compare thousands of hours of ultrasound ob-servations of individual foetuses with their emotional problems during infancy. There are now thousands of books and articles on the subject, as well as two international associations of pre- and perinatal psychology, each with its own journal (cf. Maiwald & Janus, 1993). I am here only able to summarize some of the main trends of this extensive research.

Neurobiologists used to think that because the foetus had in-complete myelination of neurones, it could not have a memory (Goodlin, 1979; Scarf, 1976; Verny, 1987). This theory has for some time been disproved, since impulses can be carried quite efficiently in the thinly myelinated nerves of foetuses, only at a somewhat slower velocity, which is totally offset by the shorter distances travelled (Anand & Hickey, 1987), thus allowing for both foetal memory and organized activity of the brain in the womb. In fact, we now know that our nerves continue to myelinate all our lives, which does not prevent us from learning during our earliest years. Far from being an unfeeling being, the foetus has been found to be exquisitely sensitive to its surroundings, and its early experiences have been found to be recorded in the early neural network—an *emotional memory system* centring in the amygdala, quite distinct from the *declarative memory system* centring in the hippocampus that is established in later infancy (LeDoux, 1994). These early emotional memories are, as psychoanalysts have long believed, usually unavailable to conscious, declarative memory recall, so early fears and even defences against them are often only recaptured through body memories and by analysing the consequences of trauma (Damasio, 1994; van der Kolk, 1988).

By the end of the first trimester, the foetus's nervous system is so well developed that it responds to the stroking of its palm with a light hair by grasping, of its lips by sucking, and of its eyelids by squinting (Bradley & Mistretta, 1975; Humphrey, 1970). It will jump if touched by the amniocentesis needle and turn away from the light when a doctor introduces a brightly lit foetoscope (Goodlin, 1979). By the second trimester, the foetus is not only seeing and hearing, it is actively tasting, feeling, exploring, and learning from its environment, now floating peacefully, now kicking vigorously, turning somersaults, urinating, grabbing its umbilicus when frightened, stroking and even sucking its placenta, conducting little boxing matches with its companion if it is a twin, and responding to being touched or spoken to through the mother's abdomen (Brazelton & Cramer, 1990; Ianniruberto & Tajani, 1981; Liley, 1972; Piontelli, 1992). If a boy, the foetus even has regular erections of his penis, coinciding with REM sleep phases; there is even evidence that baby girls have sexual arousal during REM sleep (Efron, 1985; Wolff, 1966).

The source of foetal emotions

Maternal emotions are transmitted instantly to the foetus. Lieberman found that when a pregnant mother was offered a cigarette after having been deprived of smoking for 24 hours there was a significant acceleration in foetal heartbeat even before the cigarette was lit (Lieberman, 1983), while others have shown the foetus sensitive to a wide range of maternal emotions and, of course, any drugs or other physical traumas she endures (*Child at Risk*, 1980; Norwood, 1980). When the mother feels anxiety, alterations in neurotransmitter levels are communicated to the foetus, and her tachy-cardia is followed within seconds by the foetus's tachycardia; when she feels fear, within 50 seconds the foetus can be made hypoxic, or lacking in oxygen. Alterations in adrenaline, plasma epinephrine and norepinephrine levels, higher levels of hydroxycortico-ster-oids, hyperventilation, and many other products of maternal anxi-ety are also known to affect the foetus directly. Ultrasound studies now record this distress clearly, as the foetus thrashes about and kicks in pain during hypoxia and other conditions. One mother whose husband had just threatened her verbally with violence came into the doctor's office with the foetus thrashing and kicking so violently as to be painful to her, with an elevated heart rate that continued for hours (Sontag, 1965). The same wild thrashing has been seen in mothers whose spouses have died suddenly. Maternal fright can cause the actual death of the foetus, and the death of the husband and other severe emotional distresses within the family during the mother's pregnancy can be associated with foetal dam-age in large samples in several countries (Goodlin, 1979; Stott, 1977). Marital discord between spouses has been correlated "with almost 100 per cent certainty . . . with child morbidity in the form of ill-health, neurological dysfunction, developmental lags and be-haviour disturbance" (*Child At Risk*, 1980, p. 16).

In fact, maternal emotional stress, maternal hostility towards the foetus, and foetal distress have been statistically correlated in various studies with more premature births, lower birth weights, more neonate neurotransmitter imbalances, more clinging infant patterns, more childhood psychopathology, more physical illness, higher rates of schizophrenia, lower IQ in early childhood, greater school failure, higher delinquency, and greater propensity as an adult to use drugs, commit violent crimes, and commit suicide (Barrett, 1982; Chamberlain, 1993a; *Child At Risk*, 1980; Ferreira, 1960; Herrenkohl, 1982; Mednick, 1971; Stott, 1973; Ward, 1991). Children of mothers who do not want to have them and who have experienced birth complications are four times as likely as teen-agers to commit violent crimes than are children in control groups. Suicide patterns conform to this finding: epidemiologists have found higher suicide rates in areas that a few decades earlier had had higher birth injuries (Jacobson, 1988). Other studies have shown that even the *types* of suicides were correlated with the kinds of perinatal traumas—asphyxia during birth leading to more suicides through strangulation, hanging, and drowning, mechanical trauma during birth correlated with mechanical suicide elements, drugs given during birth being correlated to suicide by drugs, and so on—so that, for instance, the rise in adolescent drug addiction and suicide recently is now believed to be at least partially due to the more active use of drugs by obstetricians during birth in recent decades (Jacobson, 1988; Roedding, 1991; Verny, 1989).

Far from being the safe, cosy haven to which we all supposedly want to return, the womb is in fact a dangerous and often painful abode, where "more lives are lost during the nine gestational months than in the ensuing 50 years of postnatal life" (Stevenson, 1977, p. 3). Few foetuses, for instance, escape experiencing painful drops in oxygen levels when the mother is emotionally upset, smokes, drinks alcohol, or takes many other drugs. As the placenta stops growing during the final months of pregnancy, it regresses in efficiency, becoming tough and fibrous as its cells and blood vessels degenerate, and it becomes full of blood clots and calcifications, making the foetus even more susceptible to hypoxia as it grows larger, thus making the late-term foetus "extremely hypoxic by adult standards" (Bartels, 1970, p. 47). Furthermore, the weight of the foetus pressing down into the pelvis compresses blood vessels supplying the placenta, producing additional placental failure (Briend, 1979). Practice contractions near birth give the foetus periodic "squeezes", decreasing the oxygen level even further (Barcroft, 1947, p. 209), while the birth itself is so hypoxic that hypoxia of a certain degree and duration will occur in most deliveries, not just in the more severe cases. The effects on the foetus of this extreme hypoxia are dramatic: normal foetal breathing stops, foetal heart rate accelerates, then decelerates, and the foetus thrashes about frantically in a life-and-death struggle to liberate itself from its terrifying condition (Boylan & Lewis, 1980; Lewis & Boylan, 1979; Wood, Walker, & Yardley, 1979). So terrible is this struggle that I have speculated that in the womb and during the birth the foetus imagines that there is a *poisonous placenta* that denies it life-giving, oxygen-rich blood and recirculates the foetus's own body poisons rather than cleansing them, as does the *nurturant placenta*. I have further speculated that the foetus thrashing and kicking out is involved in a *foetal drama* involving an imagined battle with this poisonous placenta, as a prototype for the battle with the punitive superego and all later battles with persecuting enemies (deMause, 1981).

The reality of foetal memory

That the foetal memory system is sufficiently mature not only to *learn* in the womb but also to remember prenatal and birth experiences is confirmed by a growing body of experimental, observational, and clinical data. For instance, neonates can pick out their mothers' voices from among other female voices and respond differently, with increasing sucking on a dummy, to familiar melodies they had heard *in utero* (DeCasper & Fifer, 1980; Fifer, 1987; Goodlin, 1979; Verny, 1989). As evidence of even more specific memories, research scientist Anthony DeCasper had 16 pregnant women read *The Cat in the Hat* to their foetuses twice a day for the last six weeks of their pregnancy (DeCasper, 1984). When the babies were born, he hooked up their dummy to a mechanism that allowed them to chose one of two tape recordings by sucking slowly or quickly, choosing either the tape in which their mothers read the familiar *Cat in the Hat* poem or a second tape, where she read another poem with a different metre. The babies sucked so as to switch over to the tape of their favourite poem, indicating their mastery of the task of remembering complex speech patterns heard only *in utero*.

With the number of recent experiments demonstrating foetal competence, classical conditioning, and more advanced learning ability (Carter-Jessop & Keller, 1987; Chamberlain, 1992; Osterweil, 1990; Spelt, 1948), it is not surprising that parents have recently begun to make their foetus a member of the family, playing with them, massaging them, and calming them down when they thought they communicated distress by excessive movement and kicking, and trading light pokes in return for foetal kicks, in what they call "the kicking game" (Stainton, 1985; van de Carr & Lehrer, 1992). One father taught his baby to kick in a circle; a mother played a nightly game where she tapped her abdomen three times, and the foetus bumped back three times (Stainton, 1985). Another father, who called out "Hoo hoo" next to the womb nightly, found his child pushing with a foot into his cheek on whichever side he called; father and baby played this game for 15 weeks, and he found his next baby was able to learn the same game (Freeman, 1987). These parents tried to avoid maternal stress, loud arguments, and loud noises—especially rock music—because they became aware that such sounds usually produced foetal distress.

Recent insights into foetal learning have led to some impressive research on foetal enrichment that demonstrates that prenatal and perinatal stimulation produces advances in motoric abilities and intelligence that last for years. Experimental groups of pregnant women and their foetuses who participated in prenatal and perinatal stimulation enrichment were investigated in parallel with carefully selected control groups not involved in any prenatal programme. The postnatal evaluation of both groups on standard developmental tests showed significant enhancement from foetal sensory stimulation in motoric performance, visual skills, emotional expression, and early speech (Blum, 1993). Even more impressively, when these prenatally induced enrichment effects are consolidated by immediate postnatal enrichment experiences—called "cumulative phases" by Blum, who says that they are comparable to the last stages in puzzles, when elements can be positioned easily when preparatory work has been done—they produce improvements over the control group in Stanford Binet IQ tests *at age three*, ranging from 38% for language and 47% for memory to 51% for social intelligence and 82% for reasoning: a Head Start programme of astonishing efficiency.

Ultrasound research

Perhaps the most impressive observational work on the personality of the foetus has been done by the Italian psychoanalyst, Alessandra Piontelli, who combined thousands of hours of ultrasound observations and clinical psychoanalytic work with young children. Her research into prenatal and perinatal memories began after she had encountered an 18-month-old child whose sensitive parents reported that he was incessantly restless and unable to sleep. Piontelli recounts the case:

I noted that he seemed to move about restlessly almost as if obsessed by a search for something in every possible corner of the limited space of my consulting room, looking for something which he never seemed able to find. His parents commented on this, saying that he acted like that all the time, day and night. Occasionally Jacob also tried to shake several of the objects inside my room, as if trying to bring them back to life. His parents then told me that any milestone in his development (such as sitting up, crawling, walking, or uttering his first words) all seemed to be accompanied by intense anxiety and pain as if he were afraid, as they put it, "to leave something behind him." When I said very simply to him that he seemed to be looking for something that he had lost and could not find anywhere, Jacob stopped and looked at me very intently. I then commented on his trying to shake all the objects to life as if he were afraid that their stillness meant death. His parents almost burst into tears and told me that Jacob was, in fact, a twin, but that his co-twin, Tino, as they had already decided to call him, had died two weeks before birth. Jacob, therefore, had spent almost two weeks *in utero* with his dead and consequently unresponsive co-twin. [Piontelli, 1992, p. 18]

According to Piontelli, the verbalization of his fears that each step forward in his development might be accompanied by the death of a loved one for whom he felt himself to be responsible produced marked behavioural changes. More recently, Leah LaGoy (1993), an American psychotherapist, documented 17 children who were her patients who had lost a twin *in utero* and who lived in continual fear for their own lives because they believed their mother might try to get rid of them too.

Piontelli, like many other child psychotherapists, began to be struck by the frequency and by the concreteness of children's so-called "fantasies" about their life before birth. Unlike most psychotherapists, who, however, ignore their accurate observations because their training has taught them that the mind begins only after birth, she carefully recorded these fantasies and tried to confirm their reality, first by consultation with the family and then through her own extensive ultrasound observations of foetal life. The correlations and continuities between foetal experiences and childhood personality "were often so dramatic", she says, "that I was amazed that I had not been more aware of them at the time"

(Piontelli, 1992, p. 15). One pair of twins often stroked each other's heads in the womb through the dividing membrane; at the age of one, they could often be seen playing their favourite game of using a curtain as a kind of membrane through which they stroked each other's heads. Another set of twins—whose mother considered abortion because of her fear that they might be jealous of each other—punched each other all the time in the womb and continued to do so after birth. One foetus, who often buried his face in the placenta as if it were a pillow, as a child insisted that his mother get him a pencil case shaped like a pillow that he used similarly. Still other children played out various obstetrical distress problems in later life in dramatic detail, such as one child who had nearly died because her umbilical cord had been tightly knotted around her neck and who spent most of her early childhood wrapping ropes, strings, and curtain cords around her head and neck (Piontelli, 1988). The enormous importance of being able to use foetal insights such as these in the therapy of both children and adults for profound relief and personality change has been carefully documented by Piontelli and many other therapists (Blum, 1993; Chamberlain, 1988; Fodor, 1949; Grof, 1985; Janov, 1973; Maiwald & Janus, 1993; Osterweil, 1993; Rascovsky, 1977; Schier, 1993; Share, 1994; Subbotsky, 1993; Verny, 1987).

Foetal emotions

Thus by the time we have been born, we are each an individual, having experienced the peculiar rhythms, feelings, and events of our mother, being active when she is, sleeping when she does, becoming more alert when she is dreaming in REM sleep, smoking when she smokes, being hurt by her feelings of rejection, sensitive to her every emotion because we share it in our blood. All the deepest, simplest, and most powerful emotions—the basic emotions of all religions, those that remain basic though wordless all our lives—are already felt towards our first love-object, the placenta: *adoration* of its life-giving powers, *fear* of its ability to inflict pain, *submission* to its arbitrariness, *gratitude* for the restoration of its nurturance. Every sacrificial crisis we encounter as a society, particularly war, repeats the foetal drama of a paradise lost, of being sucked into the whirlpool and crushing pressures of birth, of fighting the placental dragon–monster and of emerging into "the light at the end of the tunnel" to a new life (deMause, 1981). As Chamberlain puts it:

> *The womb is a school, and all babies attend.* It is a fact of life. The practical questions to ask are "How bad or good is the school?" and, perhaps more important, "Do you learn to love the teacher?" [Chamberlain, 1993b, p. 416]

CHAPTER FOUR

Mother–infant psychotherapy: a classification of eleven psychoanalytic treatment strategies

Stella Acquarone

I n this chapter I describe the wide range of psychotherapeutic interventions with parents and infants who are experiencing difficulties in their relationships or in themselves. For this purpose I introduce the theme from its clinical and social observation perspectives and then describe the setting-up of a project, the Parent Infant Clinic, followed by the theoretical background. Specific psychoanalytic instruments are explored, concluding with a description of the different kinds of intervention, arranged according to various client groups.

There is a group of children who, from birth, are reported to have difficulty in thriving, bonding, coping with anxiety, or tolerating frustrations. The mother's attitude often contributes to the problem. The result is emotional disturbance, expressed as continuous screaming for no apparent reason, breath-holding, feeding difficulties, sleeping difficulties, or similar symptoms.

There is a common pattern in children who are referred for psychotherapy, who are receiving special education, who are in foster care, who have been institutionalized, or who have suffered from non-accidental injury. From a very early stage of their development, these children have shown symptoms that have been confirmed by one or more professionals working with them. These symptoms could include sleeping difficulties, withdrawal, hyperactivity, and so forth.

With these observations in mind and with the idea of offering early psychotherapeutic consultations or interventions to infants and their parents who have been experiencing difficulties, I visited health centres, maternity units, Special Care Baby Units, paediatric wards, and mother and baby units in prisons for three to six hours per week, over a period of fifteen years. During this time, I studied more than a thousand cases, with encouraging follow-ups from health visitors (for up to eight years). Due to long waiting lists in National Health Service facilities, constant difficulties in preserving two- to three-hour slots for prevention work within a heavy caseload, a Monday evening forum for psychotherapists and child psychiatrists was initiated to discuss cases and to provide peergroup support, as well as to promote further research and knowledge in the field. The Parent Infant Clinic, a private institution, was created in 1989, offering parents easy access to help in understanding their infants' difficulties and in finding out to what extent the difficulties might be shared by the infant and the parents' own internal infantile conflicts. The School of Infant Mental Health, an educational affiliate of the Parent Infant Clinic, launched a fouryear training course for those who wanted to specialize further in this field. The trainees, supervised by the faculty, offer free consultations or interventions. This means that parents from all economic backgrounds can have access to this form of psychoanalytically oriented psychotherapeutic help. Referrals can be self-made or arranged via a professional. In any case, the family's general medical practitioner is usually informed.

As an adult and child psychoanalytic psychotherapist, I use psychoanalytic ideas and instruments. I have to differentiate between long-term psychoanalytic psychotherapy and early shortterm interventions, including mother–infant psychotherapy. The two treatments can take place simultaneously. The relationship between mother and baby cannot wait for the resolution in the mother or father of their past conflicts. Where there is a need for both kinds of therapy, there should be two different psychotherapists. The aim of the brief mother–infant psychotherapy is to promote an understanding of, and to facilitate, normal communication and the development of emotions and relationships. The work focuses on the mental representations of mother and infant in relation to each other, and the developing internal world of the infant is explored. The brevity is due to the idea that the relationship with its difficulties has itself been short thus far, and problems can therefore be rectified quickly. Individual long-term psychotherapy may be offered to one or both parents when the psychotherapist assesses that the mother or father has become overwhelmed by past experiences. If the infant needs regular meetings with mother and psychotherapist, then a contract is agreed accordingly.

The setting is similar to a psychoanalytic one, but the work does not necessarily occur in a formal, private consulting-room. It might take place in a hospital or clinic instead. The aim is to create a space and time where emotions can be explored with free-floating attention from the psychotherapist. Factual information is requested, in order to assist the understanding of the concerns expressed and observations made in the meeting. Links are made between the fragmented data, and they are made jointly by the parent(s) and psychotherapists. Therefore, it is important for the setting to be as free as possible from distractions, such as telephones or other electronic devices that are often found in a Special Care Baby Unit or at home.

In each interview the psychotherapist tries to analyse the situation as it was presented, taking time to consider which action or comment would be most helpful, according to the feeling transmitted. Whenever it is felt that the baby has been showing signs of normal development and is being used by the mother as an excuse to talk, this will be discussed openly. It can also be helpful to include a variety of cuddly toys and test material for babies, such as bells and a salt-container with rice in it. An in-depth knowledge of nursery rhymes will also be a great help, as will getting onto the floor early on in the interview in order to be at the same level as the baby, so that it becomes clear that understanding the baby remains the focus of attention and interest.

Of the initial 670 referrals seen over ten years for six hours a week, 307 were seen at the Health Centre, 28 and 63, respectively, were seen in two different paediatric departments, 40 in the Child Guidance Clinic, and 232 at the Parent Infant Clinic.

Types of interventions

We use a particular model of mother–infant psychotherapy, as shown below. Types of interventions are presented from 11 identified groups, which overlapped the different settings.

A. Working with the mother's mental representations

These were cases involving sleeping difficulties, feeding difficulties, and failure to thrive.

1. Crisis interventions

In this group, mothers expressed feelings of being caught up in a temporary crisis, which at times seemed insoluble and sometimes led to extreme reactions in the infant. The intervention comprised one or two meetings. These cases were mostly seen once, the mother specifically saying that she wanted help for the problem that the baby was presenting. Mother (or in some cases both parents) did not show any inclination to explore aspects of their life further. I have frequently questioned whether an intervention consisting of only one meeting has any value or justification.

Vignette: Janet, 5 days old

Janet refused to breast-feed or feed in any other way. The doctor had checked that nothing was physically wrong, and mother had become very frightened.

The interview took place in a room on the maternity ward. Janet was sleeping while mother described a good pregnancy and delivery and the breast-feeding situation. Looking at the baby, the spontaneous thought that the baby had sexy lips occurred to me, and—remembering Heinrich Racker's (1968) idea about considering spontaneous thoughts with a patient as part of a countertransference reaction—I verbalized the thought and watched the reactions.

The mother asked me how I knew just how she (the mother) felt, and, when asked to elaborate, she commented that from the moment the baby started sucking from the breast, she felt terribly aroused sexually, that she had never felt like this before, that it was unbearable, and that she feared she had damaged her daughter through her panic and despair. Once she started talking about this situation, she also talked in her native language, confusing me with a person from another country of origin—she could admit her confusion since she was experiencing so many new sensations: in her body, in her heart, and in her head. I made a link between the newborn in the mother reactivating memories; and I also mentioned possible conflicts to do with her sexuality. The mother said that sex was not spoken about in her culture; her marriage had been arranged, and she had not previously known her husband, and she did not like him. She never felt excited by him in the way she was when breast-feeding. I said that we could talk about sexuality, and I wondered whether the baby herself was puzzled and trying to make sense of the world. On the other hand, the real newborn might be experiencing difficulties as well: she might feel as puzzled as mother was in accepting all the body sensations and the sensual stimulation.

By this time, the baby had woken up, and the mother mentioned her fear of damaging the baby. On being asked whether she thought the baby felt the damage, she replied that she did. Encouraged to feed her baby and share her feelings, she did so, in spite of her doubts as to whether she was liked and wanted by the baby. I put into words what the baby might be thinking, such as: "Mummy, I feel strange sensations in my body, heart, and mind; what about you Mummy? We are partners, we both have new things to tell each other." The mother felt very relieved after I had begun to verbalize her anxieties about becoming a new mother. The intervention took an hour and a half, and I had follow-up from the Maternity Department and from the health visitor, who reported that mother and baby had a good growing relationship.

Discussion.   In this case, a quick, short intervention fulfilled an immediate need to connect and overcome what appeared to be an insurmountable obstacle. The psychotherapist's work in these cases usually ends after the feeling of being deeply entrenched becomes modified and the difficulties are overcome. The possibility of change is directly connected with the feeling of a crisis. Some mothers return for consultations at a later date.

2. Short insightful work

The mothers in this group were showing concern about ongoing difficulties that they had with their infants, without necessarily panicking. These types of interventions represent the largest number in the sample of 670 cases. The work usually took place over three to eight sessions, and it involved identifying and exploring the mother's own infantile emotions connected with ghosts in her past, which were interfering with the mothering of her infant in the here and now. On gaining insight, these mothers worked cooperatively with the psychotherapist towards some kind of resolution of the presenting problem.

Vignette: Sebastian, 18 months old

This particular mother was in a panic, feeling full of doubt and confusion about her son, Sebastian, starting nursery. Both parents came to the first interview, and they talked about school for the child. Sebastian's anxiety was concealed under the concern being expressed as to what was best for Sebastian academically. The parents, mainly mother, talked in a very worried but detached way about the child, going over and over the pros and cons of Sebastian going to nursery. Father appeared to be a very quiet and supportive person. Baby was playing by himself, isolated. It felt more as though the mother was ruminating about her past, though when she was actually questioned about her childhood, she said very quickly that she was brought up by her mother on her own and that she had dedicated her life to her mother to such an extent that only now could she allow herself to take a degree. Further exploration along these lines became highly rushed, and the mother kept returning to the matter of the child's immediate future regarding nursery school. Both parents answered questions about their family background reluctantly and quickly, and somehow the child's individuality was overlooked entirely. Mother, an architect, was desperate to go back to work; the father, a musician, was puzzled.

Twelve sessions took place, including two with the grand-mother and mother together. The child was taken to nursery for two weeks but did not settle. He would scratch and bite people, which was behaviour that he had not exhibited prior to attending nursery.

The mother gradually regressed into feelings that had been awakened by her child. First, she began to realize that the relationship she had with her son was almost symbiotic, just as hers had been with her own mother. Her father had suddenly left when she was aged 18 months (the same age as her son was now), and she re-experienced, in the sessions, the anguish of separation by cutting her husband off and clinging to her baby, even though she wanted to resolve the situation. Anxiety prevailed, grandmother and mother competing over the mothering of the son, overshadowed by the ghost of the abandoning husband and father, whom they had both loved.

During the seventh session mother asked for a session for only herself and her mother. They shouted at each other for the first time about who possessed the males; mother talked about the suffocating love she felt from her own mother and the fear of hurting her if she put any distance between them; and she expressed her longing for the return of her father, and how impossible it was to talk about feelings relating to father. The grandmother shouted back, surprised at her daughter's first temper tantrum, and she demonstrated her profound hatred and jealousy of her daughter, who had managed to keep her husband for 15 years. The psychotherapist verbalized very little, since the two women were realizing and acting-out then and there the baggage of emotions they had been carrying.

The tenth session was attended by mother, father, and baby. The parents had got married privately, had decided to go for a second child, and, for the first time in 15 years, they began to disclose their secrets. For example, they spoke about their fear of getting married and being abandoned by the father of the baby—that happiness would disappear, as it had happened to mother when she was a child.

The father had always felt rather redundant, since his partner had always kept her money and accounts secure and secret, and she had made decisions about the child without ever consulting him. Also, she would be the one who spoke all the time. Mother was horrified to see her own mother in herself, talking as though she was possessed by her, acting out the intergenerational conflict of revenge; the boy was scratching people's eyes and pushing and hitting children out of the sadness he felt because of not being allowed to develop his own self more freely.

The parents began to look at their child with new-found respect, seeing him as an individual, separate from the conflict that belonged to them and not to him.

Discussion.   In this summary it has been impossible to convey the full richness of this vignette. However, it does show how a current conflict with a child can reactivate in the parents unresolved past conflicts (as well as good experiences) that can interfere in their relationships with each other and with the normal development of the child. In this case, the difficulty arose 15 years after the parents had originally begun living together as a young couple and had continued to study and travel before having a child.

Sebastian was showing very withdrawn, sad behaviour, as well as the scratching. It seemed almost as if he was building a crust around himself, fed up with his individuality being ignored. The sessions had thrown up an amazing amount of intergenerational maternal psychic material, revealing the passive role the mother had taken in her infancy, and how it had taken 35 years to be able to talk about things such as the anguish that had been caused by the father's disappearance.

In the anxiety over her son, Sebastian was actively withdrawing or hitting, showing anger and worry, reacting intensely. The psychotherapy focused on these symptoms of the child, the interactions of the family and the maternal memories, and the effects these had on the child and on all their relationships.

3. Paediatric supportive work with aggressive or very disturbed mothers

The mothers in this group manifested a very angry attitude towards the psychotherapist and evoked concern in all professionals involved with them, rather than examining their own anger. These were the cases that presented the most problems for early intervention, where the psychotherapist felt least able to help and where one experienced the greatest risk of serious difficulties arising in the future. Some of the mothers even failed to attend their first appointment after agreeing to be referred. In other cases, the mothers presented a very high level of anxiety or felt persecuted. A different approach was needed, one that excluded getting too involved with the mother's psychopathology.

It was surprising that although they were not interested in gaining insight about themselves, these very disturbed mothers did seem willing to develop insight into their baby's feelings. The focus was therefore on the observations, pointing out and interpreting the infant's individuality.

Vignette: Sabina, 15 months

Mother and father, aged 46 and 50 years, respectively, were both suffering from multiple sclerosis. Father had had the condition for ten years, the mother for four. They had another daughter, aged four years. The mother looked ancient, tired, dispirited, and mistrustful, whereas the baby was bouncy and lively, demanding attention all the time.

Mother complained of the child's exhausting behaviour, saying it should be the reverse. On being asked what she meant by that, the mother explained that the child should be happy just to have two parents alive. This made the psychotherapist inwardly uneasy: were the children born to look after the parents? Were the parents aware of the children's needs apart from having parents alive? It didn't seem as if they were. The father had periods of feeling exhausted and stayed at home. Mother seemed easily annoyed and did not want to volunteer information about her childhood or family set-up: everything had been all right. "Just do your job", seemed to be the attitude.

She began by saying that she was beginning to feel murderous towards the psychotherapist, and she expressed a wish to run away from the consultation. The psychotherapist realized that it might help to focus on enhancing mother's knowledge about the child, and so she began to describe the child's actions and possible thinking and feelings by talking as though she were the voice of the child—in other words: "Mummy, I am lively and you want me to be quiet; I am trying to get as much as possible from you; I am frightened about your health and Daddy's." Mother laughed at this and said that babies did not think. Sabina stopped demanding and handed a teddy bear to mother. The mother said, "That's a good girl—I want you to be a good girl." The baby screamed and wanted to be picked up, and the mother did so. I suggested that baby actually meant "no, no, I want you to play nicely" and that in fact the baby was looking upset. The psychotherapist suggested that the girl might have felt annoyed about having to be what the mother wanted.

The girl moved uncontrollably, fighting the mother's tense grip, and the mother said she could not stand it. The clinician mentioned the little girl's fear of not being liked and her wish to be able to communicate her unease, distress, discomfort, as well as her good feelings. It seemed obvious that the girl was lively and full of frustrations with an internal persecutory mother who was not facing her limitations and expectations.

The psychotherapist continued by saying that we would sit on the floor and play. The mother did not. The therapist said: "Come on, Mummy, I like playing with you, take the telephone, ring a friend for tea". Baby was playing delightedly with some plastic rings, a little pole, and a doll nearby, and then everything began to get confused, and her game became unclear. The psychotherapist held the baby doll, gave it a cuddle, and sat it up, observing the girl's playing. Mother then expressed confusion and exhaustion, and it looked as though Sabina's game had become more frenzied than it ever was with anyone else, as if Sabina were living out mother's confusion.

The psychotherapist said that probably Sabina was feeling confused about herself and her parents and that a few sessions could help to contain this and to clarify feelings. Mother accepted, provided that the work was linked to understanding the baby; she did not want to be told anything about herself. The mother was able to hear and to understand about her daughter's individuality and needs. Indeed, she did change her ways, and the process took seven sessions.

Discussion. The mother developed her mothering of Sabina and probably of her own confused, frightened, debilitated baby within herself. This work did not develop insight into the mother's past, but it did allow her past to be relived, perhaps through learning tolerance and skill in reaching her baby. I think it demanded tolerance on the part of the psychotherapist towards aspects of the parents' relationships with their own parents that seemed difficult to change.

4. Network support or psychodynamic network assessment

This group consisted of mothers who were too mentally ill to cope with motherhood but who wanted help nevertheless. They had a psychiatric history, and their babies were failing to thrive or develop appropriately. The psychotherapist had to hold several interviews in order to ascertain what would be the most appropriate referral, and to set up a professional network.

Vignette: Rio, 7 months old

Rio, a boy, was displaying social and gaze avoidance; he was also hyperactive, crawling non-stop and trying to stand up. Mother and father were professionals in their thirties, and of Turkish origin. Rio was their second child.

The mother, a hitherto undiagnosed chronic manic-depressive, wept during the consultation, feeling rejected by her son, exhausted, and unwilling to do any housework. She had been in this state of extreme depression for the last four months, according to her husband, who accompanied her to the first interview.

Mother was also drinking heavily. Though concerned, father was avoiding coming home early.

Rio's brother, five years older, was refusing to go to school. Mother showed that she had the wish and the ability to try to get to know her baby's individuality but failed to understand it, no matter how hard she tried to be more alert to the baby's preferences. Clearly, she was finding it difficult to link thoughts, to identify with the baby and his needs, and to satisfy them accordingly. Her excessive crying and her inability to verbalize her feelings or to examine her past alarmed the psychotherapist. Mother could only talk about her inability to do things and how she could not understand people's feelings or what went on in their minds—including her baby's mind. Home videos of the baby from birth to two months showed a very quiet baby who, right from the start, did not engage or seek attention, already suggesting gaze and social avoidance. It seemed that a vicious circle had clearly been established: a chronic manic-depressive mother with a fragile infant who was not very interested in people or found them frightening and overwhelming.

Mother attended the third interview quite drunk, having driven for 30 minutes to get to the consultation. The psychotherapist felt that the mother should be helped to see an adult psychiatrist to take care of her own mental and physical state, but she remained totally resistant to the idea. They also discussed the prospect of her mother, who was concerned about the situation, coming to stay with the family in London if needed. In the meantime, Rio was relating to and playing with the psychotherapist and the mother, reassuring the mother about the baby's ready acceptance of her, but she, herself, could not help crying and being miserable. Since I felt that the baby and she were in danger, I firmly requested a psychiatric consultation.

The mother was eventually diagnosed as manic-depressive, was prescribed medication, which she took, and both mother and father were seen for four weeks, once weekly, by the psychiatrist, in order to monitor the effects of the medication. Thereafter, psychodynamic individual support work with the mother took place in her meetings with the psychiatrist, whereas I, the psychotherapist, had meetings with mother and baby, in order to help both the baby and the mother–infant relationship to develop healthily. Twelve fortnightly sessions took place.

The mother's mother came to London for two months; she stayed with the family and attended one interview when she first arrived in the country, in order to gain some insight into the situation. She played with the baby in the interview. The psychotherapist explained to the grandmother that the mother should be included and should be encouraged to participate more and more. Feelings of acceptance and understanding rather than criticism were discussed. The relationship between mother and baby improved by the time Rio reached the age of 13 months, and different feelings developed. The mother was now increasingly able to start feeling strong, loving and loved, interested in knowing what she felt and what her children, mother, and husband felt. The child behaved in a calm way. He played, made eye contact, and showed determination in getting his message across. He built a secure attachment to mother, and he enjoyed socializing with her.

Discussion. When a symptom in the child is present in the consultation and the mother is showing signs of unsafe and/or psychotic behaviour, it is necessary to monitor the deterioration and/or degree of risk to the child within the situation. It is also important to think with both the family and the psychiatrist about ways of measuring the seriousness of the mother's mental state and also about what kind of help is needed, rather than collude with it or escape from it as a result of internal objects in the patient being projected into the psychotherapist and the patient not being able to think them through. Here, it was necessary to allow the psychotic state of fragmentation to be held together, to face up to the underlying anxieties, and for help to be given, to be received, and to be integrated. In these cases it is important to form a network, including the father and any other willing members of the family, as well as professionals from a mother-and-baby unit or those in the community, Social Services, and Health Services. The role of this network is to think and plan together an effective support for an extremely disturbed mother–infant relationship and to enable the psychotherapeutic work to take place, allowing the child to grow, and to develop emotionally in a good-enough environment.

B. *Working on the interaction: mismatch of personalities*

Within this group there were parents who shared a common interest and who had an infant with quite a different preference or aptitude. The parents within this category that I have seen have brought their children for consultation at around two years of age, with severe symptoms such as pulling out their own hair, making themselves bleed, head-banging, or being socially withdrawn. It seemed as though the symptoms had to become severe before the parents could become at all aware of any need for help.

After an initial meeting with parents and child, I would hold two meetings for assessing the need for individual psychotherapy. Once the recommendations had been discussed with the parents, they were willing to accept the individuality of the child and to make changes within the family in order to accommodate the child who had been effectively left out. "Working with interaction" meant that, apart from just working with the behavioural interactions, we also had to think, understand, and work on the psychodynamic transactions that had to be made in order to incorporate the new member of the family.

Vignette: Andrew, aged 2 years

This little boy was brought for consultation due to his withdrawn behaviour and hair-pulling. Both parents were gym teachers and members of a sports club, and they would spend all weekend playing sports and socializing. Andrew's five-year-old sibling had flourished. In the interview, the elder child and parents played, laughed, and communicated with each other, while Andrew remained quiet and had to be drawn into the situation. He seemed bothered by the noise and preferred to go to one side and play on his own with a car.

The psychotherapist saw Andrew twice on his own; he had a calm attitude, was willing to engage, and he smiled when acknowledged, or when he changed from one game to another. From time to time, he would lie on the couch and hum nursery rhymes to himself, sometimes stopping so that the psychotherapist would continue the tune. When she stopped, Andrew would take over the tune, and so on. In the second session, his eye contact, confidence, and capacity to develop his games had all improved, and he showed no anger or frustration.

In an interview with just the parents, the psychotherapist spoke about these two sessions with Andrew. They showed interest and a willingness to discover more about his individuality, and they realized that they had been unable to imagine that a child of theirs could be so different: averse to rushing in the mornings and sporty weekends. They thought about ways of incorporating him in their routine and how to "discover" him.

The psychotherapist raised the possibility that their original "blindness" towards their son might have resulted from the fact that they were basically intolerant of difference and what that meant and why. The parents talked a great deal about how important and happy was the choice of partner to share the same interests and their wish for the children to have the same interests—a "cosy" family plan. One month later, the family interview was quite different. There had been incidents where compromises had had to be made to accommodate the second child, who was slow, dreamy, and musical, as well as changes to accommodate the older sibling's jealousy of and resentfulness at the attention now being paid to his younger brother, who was no longer showing any obvious signs of disturbance.

Discussion.   The parents' narcissistic choice of partner indicated that there might be a low tolerance to difference. However, once this was pointed out, they were prepared to accept this as a possibility, and they were willing to try different ways of communicating with their child.

These cases surprised me because of the degree of disturbance that the children had to reach before being taken to a consultation, and the quick change that occurred once this was described. I wondered whether while they are newborns and early infants, these babies do perhaps manage to form stable object relations, which help them to protest violently once they reach toddlerhood and are expected to perform differently, and it becomes possible to transmit their message clearly.

C. Work focusing on the infant

This work involved looking at the child from the point of view of his transient psychic organization at a given developmental stage.

1. Babies that are showing a developmental crisis

In fact, the crisis may be a healthy response that is transient, and the mother may need to be reassured that the child is changing internally and that he or she is letting her know this.

Vignette: Tobias, 8.5 months old

Tobias screamed whenever he woke up in a different room in a friend's cottage, or if he was held by a stranger. He had not reacted like this previously.

In the interview, the child's play and interactions with his mother seemed rich, varied, and relaxed; but with the psychotherapist, the child showed caution, scrutinizing her face and showing age-appropriate anxiety. He examined toys, and he handled keys. His behaviour was explained to his mother, and we discussed how to help the transition throughout this stage by preparing the child for nights out in the countryside or other unfamiliar events. Though mother felt that the child was too young to understand, it did make sense to her, and she was prepared to do this preventative work. She was given an appointment for a month later, though she could contact the clinic before this time if she became worried; it did seem that their attachment was secure.

In general, such cases are dealt with by the primary healthcare givers.

2. Reactive disorder: the child screams only at night

These infants seem to be reacting to a traumatic family event—for example, when mother goes back to work or when a grandmother dies.

Vignette: Suzanne, 6 months old

Suzanne had been a planned baby, the pregnancy and delivery had been good, and the breast-feeding had been wonderful for four-and-a-half months, at which time the baby readily accepted the withdrawal of the breast and the mother's return to work. This had been the plan, and great pains had been taken to find a suitable nanny. However, the baby began screaming at night, wanting only mother and breast.

Mother was exhausted in the consultation, since she was working all day and attending to the child all night. The psychotherapist asked about her feelings about going back to work, and the mother quickly answered that she was very satisfied with the domestic situation, including the baby-care arrangements.

The baby, meanwhile, seemed very content, playing with keys and rattles. There was a sense of not being allowed to talk of sadness and loss. The fact that perhaps the baby was sad and could not so easily accept the change seemed unthinkable. It seemed difficult to imagine that the mother could be missed. The mother said, very rationally: "So, what can I do? She doesn't understand the economic reasons for having to go back to work." The abrupt answer, avoidance, and the countertransference indicated an unplanned, unresolved attachment to the baby for which there had been no space. The work had to focus carefully at the level of acknowledging new feelings and experiences by indicating that perhaps there was a part of the mother that needed and wanted to be with her adorable, cosy baby whom it was unbearable to leave behind.

The baby asked to be cuddled, and mother did so. Mrs B said that she had to work, and she asked whether the psychotherapist would please help the baby to sleep at night. The baby stiffened and began to whine. I mentioned that the baby was comfortable to be with her mother when she was trying to understand the situation, but that she became tense when the mother vocalized the situation so stiffly.

I raised the question as to whether sadness was allowed from either of the parents, and whether Suzanne would be allowed to cry while mother was preparing to leave for work. Mrs B said that she would not be able to leave the house if the baby were to cry. I suggested that Suzanne might be reacting at night because she could not show her feelings during the day, and that it was a healthy reaction for both of them to be sad when separating; this sadness could be kept in mind and shared, even if it did hurt. Mrs B. said that she would be unable to keep this in mind, and that she would not be able to work. We explored the theme further. In the second session, both mother and baby were quite depressed. I felt that this was a healthy change. Suzanne was behaving like a newborn baby, and the mother was angry with the psychotherapist.

What seemed to have been transferred to the psychotherapist was a need for a mother who could take in and contain sadness and frustration, as well as smiles and contentment. There was also a need to help integrate the stage that she was going through by understanding her internal state and by sharing it with her mother, emotionally and verbally. The timing of the event, the actual leaving for work, with the previous detachment and denial of feelings, seemed to prevent Suzanne from reaching the "depressive position" wherein positive and negative aspects of mother are integrated in one person. This could be reassuring in the sense that mother was felt to be always there, and that she could be unreliable and persecutory at times and at other times very much loved and wanted.

The mother's more open expression of anger aroused in her the fear of damage to her daughter. The mother experienced this as persecutory, and she feared losing control of her new emotions and other new experiences in the world. Mother realized that she could be annoyed with the psychotherapist for opening up painful areas, and that some old feelings had been reactivated in this new state of motherhood. She was invited to explore this further.

I felt that there were two babies: the real one struggling to integrate and to feel at ease internally and the one in the mother who was feeling persecuted with the fear of losing control of the perceived stability of her plans. The adult part of the mother was available, however, to listen and to accept both babies and to continue the thinking at home. We then explored Suzanne's message of experiencing the mother as capable of taking in her true feelings—her weaknesses as well as her strengths. Before, she might well have experienced her mother as feeling too persecuted, too preoccupied with the idea of having to go back to work, not feeling attached, and having to build a false image of Suzanne, that could put up with everything until it became insupportable. I suggested to the mother that she might allow herself to think about and tolerate the experience. Mother cried, and she thought more about Suzanne's feelings in what seemed like a state of reverie, during which time the infant became relaxed, patting the mother.

From the third session, the infant slept through the night, and mother continued to think about the changing experiences with her baby and about motherhood as a dynamic process rather than as a plan to be followed rigidly. Suzanne displayed different behaviours in the interview towards the psychotherapist and the mother; these were then taken up and enjoyed by the mother, and she talked about the new feelings she had, and of the richness of the baby's personality.

Discussion.   The baby complained only at night and showed perfect adaptive behaviour during the day and in the interview. This is a common pattern among certain babies who scream only at night. It seems that they cannot fall asleep or stay sleeping because they have undigested experiences that prevent the process of wish-fulfilment through dreams, and feelings of connectedness with an internal safe, positive experience. Therefore, it is important for the psychotherapist to find out this process by accepting it in the consultation and by observing the infant's behaviour and emotions transmitted, and to be able to explore with tolerance, to share, and to understand the infant, in order to create a space in which the mother can enter, even when her negative transference is being worked out. It is, in fact, an opportunity for emotional development to resume its healthy course. Thus, it would appear that it is healthy for the baby to complain, since, if it is persistent enough, it forces the parents to seek a solution.

3. Psychosomatic disturbance

In these cases, babies may hold their breath, generally fail to thrive, have eczema, or vomit—symptoms that seem to have no physical cause. It appears that the babies are seeking the mother's attention. This may be due to depression or excessive worry in the mother. The difficulty lies in the fact that the infant's trouble has passed from the unconscious mind into the body. Parents panic, and it is necessary to find out what message is being transmitted by the baby to the mother/parents.

Vignette: Matias—15 months

Matias was the fourth of five children, all under the age of six years. He would hold his breath and turn blue, and mother was afraid that he would die. A fifth child had just been born. Mother had also come from a large family of nine children, and she had been used to children, but Matias, with his breath-holding was very worrying, and he could not be ignored.

During the interview, all four children were scrambling about and playing all over the place, even Matias; but when the baby cried and was breast-fed, he stopped what he was doing, and he started to observe, looking sad—as though he had irretrievably lost something wonderful. Father talked to me or looked at the children, but not at Matias. I said that Matias wished that he could be the baby; he wanted to have and keep his Mummy all to himself: how sad he was. He went to the teddies, and he threw one around. I continued, saying that Matias might want to do things to the baby, swing him around and get rid of him. Matias continued to knock the teddy around. When the mother asked if this was really so, I drew her attention to his look of immense sadness and longing. Mother explained that they were going on holiday to grandmother's home, and she would try to give him some more time. On their return, the mother reported no further incidents of breath-holding until two days before coming to the interview. Again, we used the session to try to understand Matias's communication of his needs. We also thought about whether it was a good idea for me to come a few more times without Matias having to display breath-holding in order for mother to understand the child's individual needs: she was not used to an approach of this kind.

Discussion.   Physical symptoms without actual physical cause require thorough paediatric investigation. It is interesting to discover and translate the message to the mother when the message contains boredom, or fear of the mother's mental state; it is important to reflect back to the mother how difficult it is for her to tolerate this non-verbal communication and to help her to examine the nature of the difficulty.

Eczema can be caused by a food allergy, but it may also be a condition signalling a growing state of depression in the mother, which causes the child to feel unheld in her mind, thus producing an irritation in the baby that is equivalent to the irritation being experienced in the mother. In babies who fail to thrive, a similar internal process occurs, whereby there is a difficulty in integrating experiences owing to a faulty attachment with mother, or no attachment with mother: she is mentally and emotionally unavailable. The infant feels dropped, unheld, uncontained, which is somatized with varying degrees of severity. My approach is to draw mother's attention *concretely* to the child by observing him, both visually and emotionally, thereby gradually promoting the kind of specific attachment needed by this particular child.

4. *Infants who find it difficult to integrate experiences*

These infants display difficulties in organizing behaviour, either by being too organized, showing early signs of obsessive, ritualistic, or phobic behaviour, or through disintegration and chaos. In either case, the element of panic in their behaviour can appear very easily, either if the ritual is broken or if an attempt is made to pull them out of their withdrawn state.

In order to "reach" their message, their vulnerable or fright-ened self has to be shown and time has to be allowed for minute signs to be picked up and understood. Any sensory activity can be a source of information. These infants fall into two main groups:

i. Crying excessively and not smiling.   These babies show panic very quickly after reaching three months of age.

Vignette: Tommy, 4 months

Tommy cried continually, and he did not smile. His parents were mature in age, and they were artistic. He demanded to be constantly held in mother's arms in such a way that he could look around. At the slightest noise he would appear startled, turn red in the face, cry, and scream, and this was causing mother to feel increasingly frightened. He seemed to be perse-cuted by not seeing where a noise came from. He did not mind whose arms he was in, provided he was upright and had good vision of his surroundings. Paediatric examination failed to find anything physically wrong, or anything wrong with his nerv-ous system.

Mother and father each came from families of three children. There seemed to be no factors in their past history that linked up with the presenting problem. The mother, Mrs P, had started to sit the baby in front of the television, as he was getting heavy, but he cried. After a careful and detailed observation of the child's behaviours and reactions in the room with mother and myself as psychotherapist, it became clear that the focus needed to be on helping the child overcome his hearing sensitivity.

The baby seemed to be trying to control the environment visu-ally, and he would become startled at the slightest noise. His hearing seemed oversensitive, and his body was tense and watchful. I asked the mother to lower her tone until, when she whispered or sang softly to him, it had a soothing rather than an excitable effect on her baby, whose tension then seemed to ease. Since sound seems to be very loud *in utero*, I inferred from my observations in the consulting-room that the child might have had to overcome discomfort in the womb, which he continued to experience in a normal environment with normal tones of voice.

The richness of the mother–infant experience appeared to have become lost somehow. Due to the mother's lack of attunement, reciprocity, sharing, and her inability to translate for her infant the experience of an unsafe, noisy world, his feelings of persecution were reinforced through lack of being understood. The mother herself suggested that she pursue this issue at home. She would go through the house, checking out all the possible noises her son was exposed to, and their source. The point of the exercise was for her to enter her son's fears and stay with them, thus helping the child find a "container" for them and gradually form a more secure base of experience, according to his own pace and rhythm.

Discussion.   In this family, a greater value was put on visual than on auditory experience. In the interview, the baby needed the experience of showing his fears by communicating them to the psychotherapist, who, in turn, shared the information with mother, thus helping the baby to overcome the difficulty. The process of developing a more secure attachment between mother and child was also initiated.

ii. Displaying avoidance of some sort—visual, social, or other. These infants, after the age of one month, display placid, lethargic behaviour most of the day.

Vignette: John, aged 1 month

After a fortnight of wide-awake behaviour, John rejected the breast, and he tended to sleep most of the time. Though this was their third child, these parents had not experienced this kind of behaviour with the other children, and they became very worried. His muscle tone seemed to be very weak. The health visitor had given all sorts of advice, but the family situation seemed to worsen. The family background seemed supportive, even though mother had moved from her country of origin with the birth of her third child. It had been difficult at the beginning, but she was happy in England. The baby did not respond to the sound of either the mother or the siblings talking, or to any caresses. I suggested that it might be useful to try holding him and try different tones of voice, touch, and smell. Finally, after 45 minutes, John opened his eyes, and it was necessary to keep him interested. It felt as though it took longer than usual for this child to react, and that he needed more stimulation than other infants of his age in order for his interest to be held. He also displayed a reluctance to share with his siblings—as if he were, even at this early age, already jealous.

On learning all of this, the mother decided that she had to make more time and space in her busy household schedule to provide this infant with whatever it was he needed. The father understood how he could help him as well, and the child gradually recovered vitality in his muscles, became more alert, and could begin to enjoy the richness of family life, which would enhance his development.

Discussion.   John's withdrawn state had to be understood in terms of his need for attention: he was passively demanding touching, holding, and talking more than do other children. Mother, who was used to carrying the baby in a sling on her back, began to hold him in her arms, to touch, look, and mirror his identity for him. Unlike his siblings, John showed an apparently innate weakness in integrating experiences and persevering with communication.

5. Physically damaged from birth or in the first year

In children who have been damaged, one often sees a higher incidence of psychosis. This implies a double process:

a. the parents mourning the infant imagined before birth, as compared to the reality of the imperfect newborn
b. the shock and trauma after discovering this reality, or living in uncertainty for what may be months after the birth.

Vignette: Martin, 2 months old, born with Down's Syndrome

Martin cried incessantly. Mother was confused by the anxiety being expressed about the baby by professionals, and the baby being too soft to hold. The mother, Mrs G, came to the interview, wanting to have classes on how to hold this kind of baby and how to tell when his heart was malfunctioning.

Mrs G already had a five-year-old child, and a good, secure marriage, but this baby's crying was different, and it disturbed and frightened her. She claimed that she did not mind having a handicapped child, but she did mind feeling anxious and not being able to understand the baby, since she, herself, did not have Down's Syndrome.

Since none of us shared the baby's handicap, we agreed that we should be careful in interpreting the baby's communications. But how would we know whether our understanding was correct? It is generally thought that crying is a sign of distress in humans. The question seemed to be in the parents' mind whether this child was, after all, human, or whether he was an animal, a monster, or even a vegetable. His gestures, body posture, responses, and reactions were then carefully observed, and the mother was encouraged to hold the infant while we discussed how she might explore this baby's personality in spite of her fears of having damaged him and of continuing to damage him.

Similar work continued over the next four sessions, helping this relationship to grow and develop, with mother getting to know the baby, while staying with the reality of her ambivalence and guilty feelings. She could then talk about what she expected and about her horror when she heard that her newborn was not normal. She thought then that it might have been a punishment from God.

Discussion. It was important not to get into the mother's unconscious needs and wishes before helping the relationship and the attachment, as it felt more beneficial to lessen the guilt first and then to enable the process of real separation; otherwise there would be no distinction between the real and the imaginary damage. There were issues of extreme confusion arising from lack of both information and emotional support—the exploratory work of her feelings and the baby's feelings developed rapidly once a mental and emotional holding of the dyad took place.

General discussion

In difficult mother/parent–infant relationships, the description of different early psychoanalytic consultations could provide a rich framework for preventative work. It may well be that psychotherapeutic work is done on a daily basis by health workers, teachers, nurses, paediatricians, and the like. However, what distinguishes our kind of work at the Parent–Infant Clinic is that we are thinking psychoanalytically. We observe closely, and we try to understand how the parents and children think, and we monitor the processes that go on between them. We make hypotheses about the unconscious dynamics and the structure of their emotional growth, based on the behaviour observed, and how it is experienced by us as psychotherapists in the room, using the countertransference. The materials we work with are the unconscious needs, wishes, defences, fears, and anxieties of the parents and children. By understanding these, we help mother and infant to attach securely, in order to be able to separate appropriately and to form object relations that can mature. During assessment, we try in the first interview to elucidate where the pain is, what expectations there had been, whose these were and how they are not being met, when and where development became difficult, lonely, or impossible, and so forth.

In brief, I have presented parent–infant psychoanalytic consultations in which the focus is mainly on:

A. mother's/parents' mental representations:

   1. crisis interventions

   2. short insightful work

   3. paediatric supportive work with aggressive or severely disturbed mothers

   4. network support—work with psychiatric mother/parents;

B. mismatch of personalities between parents and child: insight into their individualities;

C. child's mental representation:

   1. showing developmental crisis

   2. reactive disorder

3. psychosomatic disturbance

4. difficulty in integrating experiences:

  i. crying excessively, not smiling

  ii. avoidant–sensorial–complete

5. physically damaged.

This model for psychoanalytic mother–infant psychotherapy represents work done with mothers and parents who are able to express their concerns verbally and whose mental functioning and personality structure allow a positive use of the links made by the psychotherapist of the unconscious causes of actual projections or of impeded real perception of the individuality of their infant.

However, it does not include mother–infant psychotherapy where the mother is mentally handicapped or a borderline psychotic personality; nor can the model be used where there is a psychiatric condition. In such cases, the technique has to change, and the transference and countertransference are used as indicators of the state of mind; help may be given to support the family or network to create a system for caring safely for mother and infant. It is sometimes necessary to help to develop skills in the mother according to a given vulnerability in the baby.

The above model of working only with the mother's representations when the consultation is about difficulty with an infant is inadequate, and I consider it to be a resistance on the part of the psychotherapist to confront this primitive baby's transference and its countertransference. I propose the following modifications:

The therapist forms an internal picture containing all this information and treats at the available level through

1. verbal communication to the mother

  a. of her unconscious feelings, phantasies, wishes, repetition in the transference of her past experiences;

  or b. of feelings in the baby demonstrable at the time—both on his own and with the mother—which the mother has not perceived;

  or c. describing and evoking feelings that are in the air—almost as if one were dealing with two infants;

or   d.   describing reciprocal behaviours within the relationship;

or

2.   direct communication with the baby

    a.   at a sensory–tactile level to find individual aspects of the personality that need help at that moment in time;

    b.   at a verbal level, speaking softly about what one feels the baby is feeling and observing reactions as the mother hears about it;

    c.   at a visual level, making eye contact and maintaining direct observation of the baby on his own as well as his interactions with another person.

There is direct communication with the baby, starting, if necessary, at a direct sensory–tactile level. Verbal descriptions and interpretations are formulated about the structure of the baby's inner world, ego or non-ego structure, boundaries and self-image, or primitive defensive reactions of the personality that currently need help.

Conclusion

The emphasis here has been either on the mother/parent mental representation of the child, searching into their past for the ghosts of traumas that interfere in the present relationship, or on the mismatch of expectations of parents and child, or on the child when it was apparent that there were several patterns of child vulnerability within the group, including:

a.   fragility in structuring the experience around their identity;

b.   the communication of extreme distress indicative of the direct invasion of death-like feelings in the child with a consequent fear of disintegration.

Although therapeutic success is difficult to evaluate and it may still be the case that the response to treatment depends to some extent on the event of the consultations rather than their content, I did appreciate the importance in some cases of discovering the personality of the infant, which was distinct from parental perception, and the psychotherapy had to be structured around the child's needs. This was useful when deep parental disturbance or a degree of deprivation did not allow for insight into the child's inner world, or when the child's individuality was difficult to reach or understand, producing in the parent distressful reactions that could lead into relationship or personal disorders.

CHAPTER FIVE

The wider applications of infant observation

Judith Trowell

The capacity to observe is part of our humanity. From the start, babies use their eyes, their ears, touching, holding, smelling, and tasting to explore and to make sense of their environment. But for most individuals, except for the blind, the eyes take the lead because of the complexity and subtlety of the social setting into which babies are born. They use their eyes to scan the environment to gather information; and they use their eyes to convey their feelings and their needs; and they use their eyes to take in the feelings and communications from those around them. Eye contact is one of the core means by which we communicate and build relationships, and it is a key mechanism by which we develop attachments. Gaze avoidance or an inability to sustain eye contact is an important signal about the state of the relationship or the emotional state of the individual involved. Aware of it or not, we are all using our eyes, giving out and taking in all the time.

Historical view

Certain groups of people have, since before records are available, valued observation. The North American Indians and the Australian indigenous peoples spent considerable time training their children and young people to observe in minute detail the environment in which they lived. The result was adults who could, without conscious thought, notice tiny changes that were rarely perceptible, and they could then integrate and use this information to help make decisions about sources of food, water, and danger. They were better fitted to survive than those who were unable to observe.

Awareness of the importance of this observational skill does not re-emerge so explicitly until psychoanalytic ideas developed in Central Europe. Sigmund Freud's genius lay in listening to his patients and taking what they said seriously, and it also lay in his ability to observe. He noticed body posture and every action or movement. He used all of this information as important data in his attempts to understand his patients. Of course, for hundreds of years these small details had been noticed, but what Freud was able to do was to grasp their significance as conscious and, more importantly, unconscious communications.

In his monograph *Beyond the Pleasure Principle*, Freud (1920g) describes how a small child, his grandson, deals with a separation from his mother by throwing the cotton reel on a string out of his cot and then pulling it back again. This is certainly one of the pioneering moments in the study of infant observation. Freud observed the child's behaviour in detail, and he was then able to make links with the child's emotional state and with the child's conscious and unconscious struggle to understand what was happening. The early Viennese child analyst, Hermine von Hug-Hellmuth, also took up this observational work, and she began a systematic study of infants.

In 1941, Donald Winnicott wrote his paper on "The Observation of Infants in a Set Situation". In this article, he explains how for the last twenty years he had used as part of his routine clinical assessment exactly how a baby seated on its mother's knee would respond to a bright, shiny spatula on the table in front of it. By observing the subtle differences in the behaviour of the babies and how their mothers managed them, he gained an enormous amount of information both about the baby's development level but, more importantly, about the baby's emotional state and the relationship between the mother and her child. He was then able to use this information to build up an understanding of the child's difficulties; and I would suggest that he was using both observational skill and his countertransference—that is, his conscious awareness of unconscious communications.

Winnicott (1957) followed this work up with a paper on the contribution of direct child observation to psychoanalysis. In this work, he discussed a key issue in all therapeutic work: how to make sense of the information learnt about babies and children by direct observation, and the sense made of the accounts given by analytic patients during their treatment of their early childhood experiences. He encapsulated the dilemma:

> The direct observer of infants must be prepared to allow the analyst to formulate ideas about very early infancy, ideas which may be psychically true but yet which cannot be demonstrated: indeed it may be possible sometimes by direct observation to prove that what has been found in analysis could not in fact exist at the time claimed because of the limitations imposed by immaturity. What is found repeatedly in analysis is not annulled by being proved to be wrong through direct observation. [Winnicott, 1957, p. 112]

He continued by noting that

> It will always be the direct observers who are telling analysts that they have made too early an application of their theories. The analysts will continue to tell the direct observers that there is much more in human nature than can be observed directly. [Winnicott, 1957, p. 112]

This tension was to continue as infant observation spread as a training tool for those wishing to work psychoanalytically. Observing infants and young children can teach people about child development and the early family relationships, as well as about the emotional environment. But how much does it contribute to an understanding of intrapsychic development? Winnicott clearly saw that there was a tension, but he believed that it could provide insights into both kinds of development.

Melanie Klein (1952) had also addressed this issue regarding what could be understood from direct observation and what could be understood arising from psychoanalytic work. Her work with children, particularly quite young children, led her to put forward her own very detailed ideas of intrapsychic development, and the development of child analysis did provide a bridge. Klein reflected that

> Many details of infants' behaviour, which formerly escaped attention or remained enigmatic, have become more understandable and significant through our increased knowledge of early unconscious processes; in other words, our faculty for observation in this particular field has been sharpened. . . . If we are to understand the young infant, though, we need not only greater knowledge but also a full sympathy with him, based on our unconscious being in close touch with his unconscious. [Klein, 1952, p. 237]

Training developments

While these issues were being debated, infant observation was introduced as a training tool for child psychotherapists at the Tavistock Clinic. Esther Bick (1964) recognized that infant observation taught trainees at a number of different levels. They learned about child development, family interaction, and the development of a particular family over time with the arrival of a new member. They also began to understand how emotionally powerful it can be to watch babies and small children, because of the unconscious communication that observing involves, taking in not only what is externally and visually seen, but also non-verbal and unconscious communications. They also learned that this process provoked responses inside themselves that the observer's own internal world responds to in ways that were surprising, distressing, and confusing. Issues from their own childhoods surfaced, as well as issues about their parenting of their own children. Infant observation was a very powerful emotional experience, and a very important aspect of this was teaching trainees about countertransference.

The training was based on a weekly seminar with a small number of trainees and an experienced seminar leader. Each trainee observed a baby once weekly for an hour, and they wrote this up in as much detail as possible. This was then discussed in rotation in the seminar. The baby and family observed were hopefully as ordinary as possible and were found by the trainee; this negotiation was also a key learning experience. The trainee had to find the place to be neither a friend, nor an adviser, nor a teacher, nor a therapist but, rather, someone who as a participant observer responded sensitively, but who also kept to the observational task.

It rapidly became very clear that trainees learned an enormous amount about children and families, about their own reactions, and, above all, about transference and countertransference. Infant and young child observation spread rapidly across the psychoanalytic psychotherapy trainings, though at times it failed and was found to be boring, useless, and a waste of time, pointing up the importance of skilled seminar leaders to handle the intense emotional reactions (cf. Brafman, 1988; Miller, Rustin, Rustin, & Shuttleworth, 1989).

Recent developments

There have been many new developments arising out of this growth of observation as a training tool. Observational skills are now recognized as crucial for many professionals who work with people. They can assist in decision-making by increasing understanding, whether the client be children and families, the elderly, the mentally ill, or the disabled. Observational skills are also invaluable in understanding organizations. Organizational observations as a training method are spreading for those working in the state and private sectors. The observation is recorded in detail and brought back to a small seminar group for discussion, as with individual observation.

Observational work is also now recognized as a means of predicting a trainee's potential. The capacity to observe—but particularly the extent to which the trainee grows and develops in his or her capacity to observe—is a significant indicator of that trainee's capacity to grow and develop as a sensitive, appropriately open professional in the caring professions (cf. Trowell & Miles, 1991; Trowell & Rustin, 1991).

Observation is also being explored as a research tool. To what extent can observation, for example, of a mother and her baby predict how the relationship will evolve and how the child will develop? Observation is also being used as a research tool with babies *in utero* and babies in special care baby units to try to predict difficulties in the hope that it might be possible to target cases for early interventions (Piontelli, 1992).

Specific training developments

Observation as described consists of weekly observations over a period of a year or longer. Because of the excitement and aware- ness of its potency as a training tool, other developments have been attempted. At least ten observations seemed a minimum with weekly seminars. However, some institutions have had to reduce the seminars to fortnightly and the observations to even fewer in number—sometimes to two and five visits.

But this has meant that it has been possible to offer observation training to a whole new range of professionals and to both unidisciplinary and multidisciplinary groups. Seminars have also been offered to those wanting to focus on a particular topic: chil- dren in hospital, individuals with a particular disability, children in group care (such as a day nursery), children in foster care, and child-rearing practices in different cultures.

Professionals who have close contact with their clients, includ- ing social workers, nurses, psychologists, and counsellors, have found the observation experience a revelation. Professionals who have a more arm's-length approach have reacted in a variety of ways. Medical students have found observation painful and fasci- nating. Hospital doctors show a mixed response: some find obser- vation boring and a waste of time, and they want to be doing something to change what they see as painful or distressing. Others find observing acutely disturbing: they stated that they became aware of the quality of the patient's life, and how the institution did not listen to or understand the patient. They saw some of the staff under enormous stress, trying or failing to communicate with patients, whereas other members of staff did not try at all. Many hospital doctors could not continue their observations, as they found it too distressing.

General practitioners also found observation very difficult. They found it hard to take a non-interventionist role: not to be "the doctor" but, rather, just a trainee, there to learn, though with close weekly supervision they were able to manage the task. However, some of them were unable to complete the planned number of observation visits. Mostly this was because the observation made them aware of their own childhoods or issues in their clinical work and how they functioned, which left them distressed and anxious. Recent data have suggested that some 40% of general practitioners are depressed, and that they find the stress of their work unmanageable. Observation training to help them recognize their own emotional conflicts and to understand how patients communicate their distress and conflicts unconsciously would seem hugely important. To try providing general practitioners with this skill as part of their basic training would be worth consideration.

A junior doctor decided to observe a child in a day-nursery setting. The nursery was bright and cheerful, with light colours on the wall and furniture and lots of pictures and posters, so that it felt warm and friendly. The child to be observed was a two-and-a-half-year-old girl, suggested by the nursery organizer. Both the mother and the child had agreed to the observation.

> On the first visit, the observer described a series of activities available, such as construction toys, playdough, outdoor bike, and climbing frames. The children were organized and moved through these activities by the staff. The seminar group pointed out that the child—what she liked and disliked, how she had responded to the situations—did not feature much.

> In the next observation, the doctor reported a passive child who complied with the workers, moving from one activity to the next, but in fact she sat fiddling. She did not use any of the activity material other than holding some of the bits in her hands. She did not join in the chat among the other children, although she did turn and smile from time to time. But the

observer noticed that these smiles were not directed at anyone
in particular, and no other child or staff member responded. On
only one occasion did the child approach a staff member and
try to attract some attention. She was told to go and sit down
like a good girl. She made no further attempt to interact but just
moved with the group of children, as instructed. The observer
was very distressed when this was repeated at the next observation and recalled that when this child had been suggested,
the comment had been made that she is a happy, contented
child. The observer felt that no one was noticing this child, no
one encouraged or related to the child, and that she, in turn,
seemed unable to play or interact with the children. The child
was left in the nursery all day, five days a week. The observer
felt very distressed by the child and also by memories of when
he had been cared for himself as a child. He wanted to talk to
the nursery staff and spend time with the child. This was outside the remit negotiated for the observation, and he felt unable
to continue in the observer role if he could not do anything to
change the situation.

Multidisciplinary training has also become very important with
community care for the elderly, the mentally ill, and the disabled,
and also for working together in the field of child protection. Helping professionals cooperate and work together effectively has become increasingly important. Observation seminars provide a
non-threatening way of helping different disciplines to communicate. They hear what each of the others observes and what sense
they make of it, and they also discover that they have a great deal
more in common than they had expected as they see each other's
responses to the emotional and unconscious material as it arises.
Observation seminars have proved to be a significantly effective
method of crossing barriers and developing a common language.

Arising out of these multidisciplinary projects, many of which
have now been established over some years, other disciplines have
been drawn in. A particularly challenging development has been
an attempt to involve the police. Many younger police are open to
looking and observing in a different way, not seeking evidence or
scanning for signs. It is particularly difficult for the police to expose
themselves to a process that demands that they stay with uncer-

tainty or with not knowing—one of the key observation experiences: the recognition that it takes time to be clear in one's own mind about what one is observing: "Am I observing something about this particular individual, am I observing the effects of the environment on the individual, am I observing something that reminds me of my own earlier experiences, am I observing something that reminds me of what is happening in my own life now?" To become aware that what we observe can be distorted by our own emotions is vital, because then an objective evaluation can be a possibility. But for professionals who depend on the belief that they are functioning in a rational, objective manner to have this questioned can be very difficult to manage. No wonder the police find it particularly challenging and doubt its value. A small number of them in child protection teams have joined such trainings.

> A policewoman arranged to see a boy of 18 months in the child's own home, where he was cared for by a young mother. Father worked very long hours, and he was not felt to be much of a presence in the home. He also worked some weekends, as money was difficult for them.
>
> During the early observations, the observer was very caught up in the mother's issues. The young woman talked most of the time; she was clearly lonely far from her family and very uncertain about bringing up her first child. The observer's reports were full of mother, and the child was not mentioned and not "seen" very much. An observation followed where the little boy was very fractious and difficult. He kept crying, did not play busily on his own, and would not settle in front of the television. He also refused the food offered, spitting it out and making a mess everywhere. The observer felt that the child had needed a firm hand and that he was very attention-seeking. The seminar group wondered whether he was fed up with being ignored or whether something had gone on at home before the observer arrived that had perhaps unsettled him, such as a row between the parents the previous evening, or was the child perhaps unwell?
>
> The observer found this difficult, feeling sympathetic to mother and what she had been struggling to manage. The next week

the observer arrived to find that the child was in hospital with an asthma attack that had developed following a cold. She realized that she had not properly looked at the child to see if he was well, off colour, or already ill; she had become so involved with mother that she may have missed something. The observer recognized that in other circumstances she would have seen the child as difficult or delinquent and would not have looked for ill-health or unhappiness, and that her judgement was biased. She recognized how quickly she herself made judgements and how reluctant she was to give herself time for more clarity.

Conclusion

Observational skills, where the observer uses himself or herself as a trained instrument, provide an enrichment and enhancement to professional skills that can be of enormous value. Professionals can then function more effectively, make more objective judgements, have greater job satisfaction, and suffer less burnout.

Donald Winnicott (1941) recognized the value of observing infants with their mothers in a set situation. He also saw the possibility in observation of developing understanding of intrapsychic development. Both of these have borne fruit in amazing ways, but in addition recently there has been an explosion in the use of observation as a training firstly for psychoanalytic psychotherapists and psychoanalysts but latterly for those working with people in a whole range of spheres. The development of observation as a research tool is now the challenge that brings us full circle because Winnicott, with his observations of the infant's responses to the shiny spatula, was providing us with an example.

PART THREE

CHILDREN AND ADOLESCENTS

CHAPTER SIX

From baby games to let's pretend: the achievement of playing

Juliet Hopkins

I first met Dr Winnicott in 1960, when I had the opportunity to observe him performing "snack-bar psychotherapy" (Winnicott, 1963a, p. 344): his name for the provision of the least help needed to release a child from a developmental impasse. Winnicott did this work in his role as a child psychiatrist at the Paddington Green Children's Hospital. On the day that I visited, the last child patient was what was then called "an illegitimate child"—a boy of seven years who was brought by his voluble Irish mother. When the interview with Winnicott was over, the boy ran off to the toilet. As he emerged to rejoin his mother, I was amazed to see Winnicott stand up and bar his way. I was still more amazed when, in a flash, the boy climbed straight up Winnicott, slithered over his shoulder, and ran to his mother's arms. We all laughed, and Winnicott said something about the boy's courage standing him in good stead.

Winnicott's playful use of an oedipal challenge to this fatherless boy was a startling contrast to the exclusively interpretative approach to which I had been introduced at the Tavistock Clinic. As students of child psychotherapy, we were not expected in those days to initiate play with children. Perhaps Winnicott enjoyed having presented an unorthodox challenge to me as well as to his patient.

A year later I was fortunate to have Winnicott as the supervisor of one of my training cases. As far as I know, no other student child psychotherapist ever shared this good fortune, since doctrinal differences dictated that students should be supervised only by the orthodox. However, the Tavistock Clinic training, though Kleinian in orientation, allowed some latitude to its few "middle group" students like myself to select our own supervisors. I needed my training analyst's insistence to gain the courage to approach Winnicott, and I felt overawed when he agreed to see me. My anxiety increased when he fixed a regular appointment at lunch-time and sat listening to me with closed eyes. I felt sure that he would have preferred an after-dinner nap. However, when he shared his thoughts, I found that he had not been asleep but had been listening intently. There was nothing doctrinal about his views. He never told me what to do or say. He listened and then shared his thoughts, letting me see how he played freely with alternative ideas and encouraging me to do the same. I had to tolerate much uncertainty.

My intention here is to give a brief account of the psychotherapy that Winnicott enabled me to do with a little boy who could not play. I intend to use the development of this child's capacity to play to illustrate Winnicott's thoughts on playing. In this way I hope to show the sequence of stages through which a child achieves the full capacity for playing, and at the same time to recapitulate Winnicott's own achievement: his revolutionary theory of playing.

My patient was a three-year-old boy, whom I shall call "Paddy". He had no speech, and he was not toilet-trained. His parents reported that he had never shown signs of attachment to them, and he often wandered off and got lost. He showed no awareness of danger and no response to pain, and he regularly ate dirt and rubbish. He had never learned to play, but he simply wandered about "getting into things". Paddy's birth and his early history had been normal, but his development was so slow and deviant that the referring paediatrician was uncertain whether he was mentally handicapped or psychotic.

Paddy was the only child of a very disturbed and unhappy couple. His mother was a seriously depressed and anxious woman, preoccupied with thoughts of suicide. She suffered from severe eczema, and she explained that she had always avoided touching or holding Paddy in case his germs should infect her skin. Paddy's father was a very eccentric man who read philosophy all day and had never been able to find a job. Neither parent had ever thought of playing with Paddy, and they were at a loss as to how to relate to him.

It was arranged that Paddy should come to see me five times a week—the expected frequency for child analysis in those days—and weekly casework was provided for his parents. The developments that I describe in Paddy were facilitated not only by his own psychotherapy, but also by beneficial changes that his parents became able to make.

My first encounters with Paddy were utterly bewildering. He wandered cheerfully around the room, clambered over furniture, dropped and threw toys, and made a lot of noise by banging and shouting. I found myself entirely unable to think of any of the interpretations I had been learning how to give.

Winnicott (1971a, p. 51) was later to write: "Interpretation when the patient has no capacity to play is simply not useful or causes confusion." In supervision, he warmly supported my intuitive response, which was simply to verbalize what Paddy was doing and feeling. Winnicott spoke of the importance for children of naming their emotions, intentions, and body-parts. Naming, he said, makes shared and therefore socially acceptable what previously was only private fantasy. Putting children's experiences into words gives them greater self-awareness and hence greater control; and it allows fantasy to be checked with reality, and increases the capacity to remember. It also reduces guilt. So "naming" was not simply the failure to interpret that I had feared it to be.

Since naming can elucidate latent meaning, Winnicott might well have considered it to be a form of interpretation, but, like other child analysts of his time, he reserved the use of the term interpretation for the classical transference interpretation. My Kleinian teachers believed that only transference interpretations could bring about lasting change. However, today most Kleinians (e.g. Alvarez, 1992) recognize naming as a valued form of interpretation, suited to an immature child's developmental level. Like Winnicott, Anna Freud (1965, p. 228) always recognized the value of "verbalization and clarification", but she saw it primarily as a preparation for analysis proper rather than recognizing its full therapeutic potential.

Fortunately, Paddy warmly welcomed my attempts to feed back in words what he was feeling and doing. He began to look eagerly at my face to see my interest in him reflected there. Much later, in his book *Playing and Reality*, Winnicott (1971a) described how vital it is for the infant to see his mother's face reflecting and responding to his own state of mind, not frozen or preoccupied. Paddy appreciated that my face and words mirrored his experience and so confirmed his existence. He began to talk, to point to himself when he wanted something, and to call himself "Paddy". He seemed touchingly overjoyed to discover that he possessed his own thoughts and feelings. He had arrived at feeling "I am".

For Paddy, the discovery of "I am" was accompanied by the parallel exploration of "We are". Paddy took great pleasure in having or doing the same as me. He was thrilled to discover that we both had blue sweaters, we both had buttons, and we could both draw circles. He liked to imitate me and to be imitated. We "clapped handies", blew raspberries, and made animal noises. Thus we established mother–baby games that normally originate within the first year. These games express a mutual identification in which the infant distinguishes between the "me" and the "not-me" while retaining through play the potential for assuming either the mother or the baby role. Winnicott thought that such early playfulness within the holding relationship took place in the transitional space, the overlap between mother and baby at a time when the baby was not yet fully aware of the mother as a separate person upon whom he depended. Certainly at this early stage of his treatment Paddy had not yet begun to experience me as a separate person whom he missed between sessions or whom he could imagine to have a personal life of my own.

Winnicott had observed that the development of play depends upon trust. Paddy's first venture into play with me must have been based on his growing confidence that I would continue to prove reliably friendly and emotionally available, able to respond to his spontaneous gestures.

I remember asking Winnicott how I could enable Paddy to move on to the next stage of development—surely interpretation was needed now? But no, it seemed that one form of playing could lead spontaneously to another. Playing could be both a reflection of the psychotherapeutic process and a means of bringing it about. Paddy began to pretend. His first pretend play, like that of many babies, took the form of pretending to feed me and then of inviting me to pretend to feed him. Plasticine and water became "nanas and mook" (bananas and milk), and part of each daily session became a mutual feast.

Winnicott knew that this new capacity for togetherness was essential for providing the context in which Paddy could risk discriminating and tolerating differences. Paddy started to become interested in observing and exploring my body, and he focused on differences in our clothing and anatomy instead of on our similarities. All the toys had previously been held in common, but now he selected "his" cars and bricks and he allotted the others to me. He would sit surrounded by his chosen toys and indicate that I should not let mine intrude upon his boundaries. The difference between "me" and "not-me" was becoming increasingly delineated.

During this period Paddy gradually developed a powerful attachment to me. He greeted me with enthusiasm and felt very rejected when it was time to go. Disillusionment was painful. He was forced to confront my separateness and to face his anger about it. Hide-and-seek became his favourite game. This allowed him to play out his anxieties about separation and loss of contact and about retaliation and attack. He would jump out of his hiding place to frighten me, and he liked to kick me on occasion. These games of hide-and-seek enabled me to verbalize his hopefulness that he would not be forgotten when out of sight, and that I would want to find him when he disappeared. I was becoming for him both a mental image that he could recall in my absence and a separate person in the external world who came and went.

During my supervision I gradually realized that Winnicott's approach to children's play was different from Melanie Klein's. Klein used play to understand and to interpret children's anxieties.

Winnicott did this too, but he was more interested in the way in which children themselves use play to reflect and facilitate the development of the self. He decried "running commentary" analyses, which, by verbalizing everything, steal the child's experience of his or her own creativity. For Winnicott, the significant moments in child analysis were not the psychotherapist's interpretations but the child's use of play to surprise himself or herself with new awareness, just as adults make self-discoveries by talking problems through with a friend. Winnicott (1971a) recognized that through playing, psychotherapy of a deep-going kind may be done without interpretative work. This enabled him to appreciate fully the work of play therapists.

Paddy's next forward step was his attempt to integrate his aggression through symbolic play. He intended that we should both enact crocodiles. Instead of the mutual feasting we had enjoyed, we voraciously attempted to eat each other. This play was not playful but urgent, compulsive, and aggressive. Such play is likely to be motivated by the repetition compulsion, with the aim of mastering unresolved trauma (Freud, 1920g).

It was at this point in Paddy's psychotherapy that interpretation began at last to play a significant part. When repression has rendered conflicts deeply unconscious, they cannot be spontaneously resolved through play, which may become unplayful and repetitive, as Paddy's play had become. Interpretation aims to help children to understand what they are worried about so that they can recognize it and work it through.

Paddy's crocodile play could be understood in many ways, but it was particularly meaningful to him when I likened the crocodile's scaly, wounded skin to his mother's eczema and I spoke of his feelings of responsibility for causing this. Klein had taught me that children's imaginary monsters were projections of their own aggression, but Winnicott's view that playing takes place in the overlap of the "me" and the "not-me" led me to the realization that Paddy's crocodiles reflected not only his own aggression, but also the experience that had aroused it (Hopkins, 1986). In this case, it was his mother's physical rejection of him on account of her eczema that proved problematic. Playing out these aggressive themes helped Paddy to separate fantasy from reality and to recognize that wishing to hurt is not the same as doing, and that thought is not equivalent to action. But Paddy's feelings of responsibility for his mother's eczema and for her rejection of him ran deep and proved very hard to mitigate.

Interestingly, it was after Paddy had tested my capacity to contain the crocodile's aggression that he ceased to be oblivious to physical pain. Perhaps he now allowed himself to cry when hurt because he could rely on my survival, and also on my availability to comfort him (cf. Fraiberg, 1982). After 15 months of psychotherapy, Paddy had become talkative and toilet-trained, and he would no longer eat rubbish. His parents had been greatly reassured by the improvements in his development, and he began to exhibit an affectionate attachment to them both. A nursery school agreed to give him a place, and so he gained his first opportunity to play with other children.

One of the benefits of my supervision with Winnicott was the extension of my imagination beyond the range of children's unconscious fantasies as described by Freud and Klein. For example, Winnicott was fascinated by children's response to gravity. He thought of gravity as posing a male quality to be mastered and a female quality of uniting with earth, whether in love or despair.

From early in his treatment, Paddy worked at defying gravity by erecting great piles of wobbly furniture. He wanted to put a cushion on top and sit there. Winnicott thought that Paddy was aiming to recreate mother's lap, to climb up into her arms and resist being dumped on account of her depression. Paddy was asserting his determination to keep himself up even if mother let him down. He developed games of climbing round the room without touching the floor. These games were very exciting, and here he illustrated Winnicott's (1971a) thesis that playing is inherently exciting and precarious, not on account of instinctive arousal, as Klein had believed, but on account of the precariousness of the interplay in the child's mind between what is subjective and what is objectively perceived. Paddy was excited by managing the interplay between fantasies of falling and of flying and the realities of his limited powers to master gravity. And when he mismanaged the interplay, he fell. I know that Winnicott's sensitivity to the effect on Paddy of his mother's depression was based on his own experience of a depressed mother (Phillips, 1988). His personal mastery of this childhood experience has provided us with some of his most profound insights.

Paddy had yet to achieve the capacity for role-playing. This first began at the age of four and a half years, when he called himself "King of the Castle" and called me "the dirty rascal". From there he went on to role-play various admired daddy figures: the coalman, the postman, the milkman, and the dustman. This make-believe led us into themes of oedipal rivalry and jealousy. Later he risked reversing roles with me—for example, saying: "You be Paddy. I'm you. I go home to my daddy-man and you cry." This was clearly a means of mastering his jealousy, but it was also the first step towards putting himself in another's shoes—a development that Winnicott (1971a, p. 119) later called "inter-relating in terms of cross-identifications". This represents the creative aspect of introjective and projective processes.

Paddy's capacity to verbalize his fantasies increased. When I told him of my coming summer holiday, he clutched his genitals and told me that his willy was a baby camel with two humps, which would feed him in the desert. This symbolism was meaningful to me, but Paddy's distress about my holiday ensured that he used the symbolism in a literal way: he could not allow us playful space to think about it. A year later, aged six, he remembered this fantasy with much amusement and told me: "I really believed my willy made milk! Now I pretend my willy makes me fly—but not *really*!" Paddy had now achieved both a sense of humour and a more mature capacity for playing—a capacity that Winnicott distinguished from the physical activity of play. Playing denotes the ability to distinguish reality from fantasy and past from present, while giving playful rein to a creative imagination that is neither delusional nor literal.

Today, the cognitive aspects of this development are being explored by researchers on the "theory of mind" (e.g. Astington & Gopnik, 1991). Winnicott could have told them what so far their research has ignored: that the capacity to think flexibly and imaginatively about thinking, to play with reality, depends upon a facilitating environment. In ordinary good-enough homes, this capacity develops naturally enough. But in homes where the baby finds no mutuality, where the parent's face does not reflect the baby's experience and where the child's spontaneous gesture is not recognized or appreciated, neither trust in others nor confidence in the self develops, and play is stunted. During his therapy, Paddy had gained enough trust in me to play, and he had used his play and my reflection upon it to develop a capacity both for imagination and for self-reflection. He had also developed affectionate attachments, lost his symptoms, and become able to prosper in a mainstream school. When psychotherapy ended, he was not free from problems, but he was able to cope.

In the more than three decades that have elapsed since then, children's toys and games have changed, but the way in which children use play to find and become a self remains as Winnicott described it. Winnicott was alone among psychoanalysts in recognizing that playing lies at the root of our capacity for creative living and for the enjoyment of life (Hamilton, 1981). He expanded Freud's view that mental health is reflected by our capacity to love and to work. He saw that our mental health also depends upon the establishment of a transitional realm in which subjective and objective overlap and in which all playing, all culture, and all religion belong. He recognized that our mental health depends upon our capacities to love, to work, and to play.

CHAPTER SEVEN

Psychoanalytic perspectives on traumatized children: the Armenia experience

Sira Dermen

My work with earthquake survivors in Armenia might be called applied psychoanalysis—which is true but somewhat misleading. The story starts not with professional identity, but with national identity. I went to Armenia in the wake of a major disaster because I am Armenian. That a psychoanalytic perspective was of value in the midst of the rubble of Spitak was a discovery for me; equally, that the psychoanalytic community would find my thoughts on this subject of interest.

The paper on which this chapter is based was written more than a decade ago and has been left substantially unaltered. It was read at a meeting of the Applied Section of the British Psycho-Analytical Society (September 1990); versions of it were also presented at the Tavistock Clinic Survival Seminar (May 1989), as a Freud Memorial Lecture at University College London (November 1990), and at the 37th Congress of the International Psychoanalytical Association in Buenos Aires (August 1991). I am grateful to Dr Armen Goenjian, under whose auspices this work was carried out, and to Caroline Garland, Adam Limentani, and Joseph Sandler for their encouragement at crucial points during the writing. I also want to express my thanks to the Tavistock Clinic Foundation for a grant.

My approach is personal. I have made three working trips to Armenia since the earthquake, and my vision has gradually changed. The process is best captured in a phrase of Martha Wolfenstein (1957, p. 189): "*the rise and fall of the post-disaster utopia*". Two years have passed since my first trip and I am having to face the fall of my own utopia.

This utopia was not sustained by illusions about the adequacy of the work I did there. Rather, it was associated with an intensity of personal commitment, called forth by the immensity of the suffering of the people with whom I worked. I quote again from Wolfenstein:

> There is something extremely impressive about those who have passed through a terrible danger and survived . . . this capacity of human beings to survive extreme ordeals partakes of the quality of heroism. . . . Those who have suffered extraordinary assaults . . . are apt to seem more noble than ordinary people, and to evoke the admiration and love which are the due of superior beings. [Wolfenstein, 1957, pp. 190–191]

I now write from a perspective of the gradual erosion of this original state of mind.

Nor is it just guilt: flying into a disaster area, working for a few weeks, and flying out, abandoning the people with whom I worked. What has changed has to do with truth and the loss of a sense of carrying an urgent message. When I returned from my first trip to Armenia, I felt consumed by a mission: to communicate as accurately as I could what I had witnessed and experienced there. My perspective was entirely psychological, my desire to interest colleagues in Armenia's enormous need for professional help. Two journeys later, I feel ambivalent about communicating what I saw. The truth is so complex and historically saturated, and any simplification feels like a betrayal of the people of Armenia, who have been through, and are still going through, great suffering. It is not just a question of an earthquake. It is a history of subjection to alien rule since at least the fourteenth century, a genocide in living memory—still scarcely acknowledged by the world, still denied by the perpetrator—massacres in Azerbaijan that occurred before the earthquake, and a continuing fight for national survival. But as the poet Joseph Brodsky (1987) says, "The uniqueness of the size of one's grief is no guarantee of anything, certainly not of nobility."

It has taken me three trips to discover this and to acknowledge that I am not only witnessing individual suffering, but also the burdens and distortions from past crimes and failures. I can no longer take the necessary constraints of my professional stance, which is to address only the thoughts and feelings of the individuals who come to see me, as a justification for ignoring the overall social structures in which Armenians are living their lives. If the basis of psychoanalysis is a continuous working towards the most truthful interaction possible, and if the basis of the society is manipulation, lies, betrayal of promises, then there is an inevitable and persistent contradiction.

This chapter has two pervasive themes: the discovery—surprising to me—of the applicability of psychoanalysis in seemingly unpropitious circumstances, and the unsurprising fact that psychoanalysis requires a social milieu that does not contradict its essential values. Time has passed, and everything I say is from my current perspective. So in order to give my initial response to working in post-earthquake Armenia, I include a paper I wrote soon after returning from my first trip. I treat it as a document, saving all comments for later.

The Armenia experience

I would like to tell you my story backwards; not how I got to Armenia, but how I got back from the earthquake zone to ordinary life. The major divide was not between Armenia and England. It was between Spitak, the epicentre of the earthquake, where I worked, and Yerevan, the capital of Armenia, physically untouched by the earthquake. After two weeks in the earthquake zone, Yerevan was a shocking experience. I felt an alien in this lively, seemingly carefree city, a city with its streets and buildings intact. And London: my plane landed at Heathrow, but my own personal landing was in a series of stages. Each stage corresponded to a moment of communication when a friend or colleague who had been listening to me said something that made a bridge between the two worlds. I felt that they had glimpsed that other world through my inadequate and inchoate account. I was not shut in and shut off. People wanted to know—this was my true home-coming.

For example, a friend who had listened to me for hours said: "I am reminded of the literature of the First World War. The soldiers would come back from the front, and they could not talk. They wanted to go back to the trenches. Because there people knew." By perceiving my omissions—what I did not say—he had given shape and definition to my pervasive sense of isolation. I recognized what haunted me: not only the particular individual tales of hor-ror, loss, suffering, but even more the untold tales engraved on human faces and bodies, and on the face of the land.

There must necessarily be a vast difference between my mental state and that of a soldier who has fought in the trenches or a citizen of Spitak. To ignore the difference is to abandon all sense of propor-tion and to reduce all traumas to the same size. I have sustained no loss: my body is intact; my family and friends are not dead. I have not lost my home, my place of work, my colleagues, or my patients. But I was a witness in a world where most people had lost children, parents, relatives, friends, homes, schools, teachers, hospitals, col-leagues, patients. And even that act of witnessing, that experience at one, two, three removes, four months after the earthquake, left me in a state of isolation. My theme, then, is isolation.

I will give a clinical illustration. It is, relatively speaking, one of the least tragic cases, and for that reason easier to relate. This is a boy of 11, "A", who was brought to see me because of his parents' concern that he would not speak about what had happened to him at the time of the earthquake. He was alone at home, and had been trapped under rubble for two hours before his father rescued him. His injuries were minor, and he had not been hospitalized. There had been no deaths in his immediate family. Their home was unin-habitable, and, like thousands of other families, they had been evacuated to a resort town in Russia. His father has a responsible job and had stayed behind. When I saw A, the family was tempo-rarily reunited for the Easter holidays. They were still homeless and were staying with relatives. His parents' question to me was: "Is he all right?"

I saw him in the kitchen of the flat where I was staying, while his parents and his younger brother were having a social visit with their friends, my hosts. I had put out the family of dolls and some drawing materials, which he did not touch until the very end of our session. It was hard to establish contact with him at first. He sat rigidly, and he very politely told me that he was fine. Yes, he agreed with me that there was a gap between his parents' anxiety for him and his own sense that he was perfectly all right, but he had no thoughts on the subject. I realized that he had been brought by his parents for a diagnosis of a psychological state, and so he had to say over and over that he was well. He insisted that he was not afraid, that he had not been afraid during the earthquake, and that he knew that his father would save him. He told his story factually and externally.

He was at home alone watching television, and he felt the earthquake. He tried to get out to his uncle's flat next door, but he could not open the door—then his uncle came, but he could not open the door either. Two hours later, his father got him out, having got help from the soldiers. I pointed out that he would tell me about the beginning of the two-hour period, and about the end, but not about the middle. This was true, but my observation did not get us far. His five-year-old brother walked in, obviously curious. A alternated between stroking the brother's hair lovingly and telling him off whenever he did anything spontaneous. "Don't," he said, "you mustn't", when the child touched the family dolls. I asked why. The patient, A, smiled, and, at a loss for words, he shrugged his shoulders. This introduced a lighter tone into the proceedings, a sense of A laughing at himself. When the younger child left the room, I noticed A gazing longingly at the kitchen door. I said that he would rather be with the others in the living-room and not here with me. This proved a crucial intervention. He agreed with relief. He started to talk more freely. It emerged that he had been trapped under stones and earth. He could free one hand and remove a few stones but could not move the rest. I said how awful this must have been and how he could not have known how long he had been lying there with all those stones on him. He said that he could hear his father's voice calling to him all the time, and he managed to convey how important and reassuring this was for him. With time I realized that he himself had remained silent. "I could not reply," he said. I asked why, and he said, "Because if I opened my mouth, it would fill up with earth." This was a real piece of communication; in retrospect I think it was the central communication. By now the event and his experience had come alive between us in full horror.

I said he has not been able to open his mouth ever since. I talked to him about how isolated he must feel—he was the only member of his family who had been trapped. It must be difficult for him to feel "I was trapped, they weren't", and difficult to express, for all sorts of reasons, like not wanting to upset his parents. He responded immediately by saying that he did not know who in his class had been trapped and who not. But he did know that one girl from his class had died. And then with great animation he told me the story of a boy who was also trapped. This boy loved sweets. He had gone into the larder to eat sweets, something forbidden by his mother. His sister told him not to eat sweets, and when she realized that he was not obeying her, she locked him in. The earthquake happened just then. He was trapped in the larder, a small room, but he didn't have stones or earth on him; he was free, he could walk about. They could not unlock the door. Eventually, when they did open the door, it turned out that he had not realized that an earthquake had happened—he had just been eating sweets! He was so thirsty that he had four glasses of water. At the close of his parable-like tale A was laughing with abandon in an engagingly childish way. Then, after a few moments of silence, he said, "But he could have died." I said his thought was, "*I* could have died."

This vignette reads like a detail from a session that one might have in London, except that we were in a kitchen and people were walking in and out. Apart from the open-door aspect, it was not typical of the conditions in which I worked in Armenia, which were much more chaotic.

Spitak, the main town where I worked, was literally smashed to pieces. No building was intact—ruins and rubble everywhere, and few people. Half the population had died, and many of the survivors had been evacuated. Those remaining were living in tents, while the fortunate had a temporary wooden hut. The hospital was operating from a series of trucks and tents spread around what had once been the town's football field. Spitak had had no psychological help since the earthquake. The Deputy Chief Physician of the hospital introduced me to the neuropathologist as the medical specialist closest to my area of work; and thus my main base in Spitak came to be the truck of the neuropathologist.

On my first morning a group of parents with children were waiting for me in the freezing cold. I made a rough division on the basis of those first arrivals: a group for the younger children, another group for infants with their mothers or grandmothers, and still another group for adolescents. Each group would be offered three meetings. But where would people wait? I was not to worry, the adults kept reassuring me—they would find somewhere to wait. They looked patient, fatalistic, as if being kept waiting was nothing to them. Where would I see people? The tents were large, cold, draughty, and they afforded no privacy. The neuropathologist offered me her truck because it was warm. The front two-thirds of her truck was her consulting-room, and this we shared; the back one-third was divided with a flimsy curtain and afforded some privacy. We spread a blanket on the floor, and this became my space for seeing the group of smaller children and infants with mothers. On my tiny bit of blanketed floor-space the children played with the therapy toys I had brought with me: a family of dolls, small animals, bricks, drawing materials. I worked in a non-directive way, because this is the only way I know how to work, observing what they did, how they related to each other and to me, and commenting as appropriate. I did not tell them to draw an earthquake, for instance. But with time some of the children brought earthquake-related phantasies. One boy drew a picture of a monstrous animal whose flame-like excrement had toppled over a house. And one girl stated at the end of the second group meeting, "Tomorrow will be the last, won't it?", and she then proceeded to beat up the father doll. And when I asked her to tell me what she was doing, she said, "She hates her father . . . all the children hate their fathers now."

People would arrive throughout the day. I would see them in all kinds of different combinations, depending on the circumstances, demand, and time of day. For the larger groups we had to move to a corner in the nurses' tent. Sometimes I would get a large group of 8- to 16-year-olds to play and to draw, and then I would talk to the parents. The parents would start by worrying and, indeed, by complaining about the children: "They're afraid", "their sleep is disturbed" . . . "they fight with each other" . . . "they're clinging". And with time they would slowly shift the focus to themselves: "And what about us," they would say, "aren't we afraid?", or: "I don't have my old patience any more; last night I was screaming at my children", or: "I find excuses to go into their bedroom at night to see they're all right. I can't bear to be on my own." My tentative opinion is that some at least of the children are bearing a double burden—their own and that of the adults.

I will give an illustration that makes the point all too starkly. Mrs B came to see me on my last day in Spitak. She came ostensibly to tell me about her 10-year-old daughter's symptoms. She complained that her daughter got tired very easily and could not concentrate on her schoolwork. In addition, she had developed tics again since the earthquake, for which she had in the past received in-patient neuropathological treatment. Her upper arm, neck, and head moved in uncontrollable jerks, I was told, though I saw no sign of tics as she sat there listening to her mother talking to me. At first Mrs B looked and sounded grim and complaining. With time, she told me her story. She herself had been trapped for 16 hours when the hospital where she worked as a nurse collapsed. When she was freed, she refused medical treatment, and she ran to search for her daughters. She discovered her four-year-old daughter's nursery in ruins. Scarcely any of the children survived. The body of her young child was found 45 days after the earthquake. For reasons that were not altogether clear, she had lost touch with her older daughter, who was returned to her by the militia nine days after the earthquake. The girl had managed to run out of her school building, had gone home in search of her mother, and had found their house demolished. Mrs B was getting more and more upset as the story unfolded. I said that she blamed herself for the death of her little girl. In tears, she told me that on the morning of the earthquake her four-year-old daughter had not wanted to go to the nursery. She had asked repeatedly to be taken to her mother's place of work. The mother had left the child crying and pleading not to be left. This was her last memory of her little girl. Her husband had been working in Russia at the time; he had set out immediately, reaching home three days later. He was due to leave again shortly. She expressed considerable hostility towards him: she has had to bring up the children on her own and she has had to be the responsible one. I had noticed all along something punitive in the way in which she talked of her daughter's symptoms. She said: "I want her to go back into hospital and be cured. She doesn't want to go, she doesn't want to leave me. But let her go and be cured." It was possible to do some minimal work with her, in the hope that some understanding of her guilt in relation to her younger daughter might stop her repeating the abandonment with her surviving daughter. Perhaps the hardest thing for me, listening to this tragic tale, was knowing that I was leaving and that there was no local psychotherapist to whom I could refer her.

To return to my opening theme of isolation, in talking to children, parents, and professionals, one thing that I discovered was that each had an area of guilt in which they were locked and which they had not shared with anyone: a doctor who could not reconcile himself to the fact that he had not even considered saving his patients, he had run straight to his own children's school; a young girl who felt responsible for her father's heart attack because it had occurred on his way to fetch a doctor for her; an adolescent who had left his elderly teacher alone in the classroom when he ran out to save himself. Insofar as I was useful out there, I think it was through having lessened the isolation, however minimally.

Thus isolation is doubly my theme: theirs, and mine upon returning. For if I cannot relate that world to this one, and if *I* need help from others, then we can only just begin to imagine what the people of that other world need. One thing that they need from mental health professionals is an appreciation of how difficult it may be for them to speak their experience in a meaningful way, to tell—to discover—their individual narratives.

Discussion

This is the end of the document. I have spent a good deal of time since then discovering my own narrative. I went to Armenia as a professional—specifically, as a child psychotherapist. I soon discovered that for the people of Soviet Armenia, who had received me and other colleagues with extraordinary generosity, the meaning of our visit was broader: their fellow Armenians from the diaspora had come to them in their hour of need. "We don't feel abandoned", was a constant refrain. The giving and receiving of aid in extreme situations is a highly charged emotional experience—a fact well known to workers in the field. But another well-known fact—the resistance to psychological aid—had been almost totally absent. This, I came to realize, was partly because we were stepping into a culture unused to psychologically minded professionals—where there were not only no psychoanalysts or psychotherapists, but also no clinical psychologists or psychiatric social workers or bereavement counsellors. The adults saw me, at least initially, as someone to whom they could talk about their children's problems.

It was not only Armenian relief workers who were welcome. Anyone from abroad was also welcome. Armenians felt that at long last the world was taking some notice of them. Their gratitude was boundless and moving. The culture has very high standards of hospitality. Foreign aid-workers described again and again how in the midst of devastation and chaos, in a tent, out of the rubble, so to speak, a table would be spread, and they would be fed.

The silence that I often encountered when working professionally, the sense of horror and grief beyond words, contrasted sharply with the volubility of public utterance. People were driven to talk, and one was bombarded with stories. What they wanted the world to know about was not just the earthquake but their political situation: the massacres by Azerbaijanis of Armenian civilians in February 1988—that is to say, before the earthquake—unleashed because the people of Nagorno Karabagh had taken the promise of *glasnost* seriously enough to have petitioned for union with Armenia, using entirely legitimate and peaceful means, and the failure of Soviet authorities to protect them, coupled with their subsequent unwillingness to bring the perpetrators to justice. Their hatred of Mikhail Gorbachev was the greater for having once put their trust in him.

Thus, I had to understand that although I had gone with my head full of earthquake, the natural disaster, they were equally traumatized by the political disaster. And the recent massacres had revived memories of the 1915 genocide, which claimed the lives of one and a half million of the two million Armenians living in

Ottoman Turkey. To ground this in a bit of empirical detail: when talking to me about how the earthquake first hit their senses, many survivors tried to describe the peculiar sound of the earthquake, a sort of rumbling roar, and reported their first thought as "the Turks are coming".

A genocide or massacre contrasts with a natural disaster in that there is somebody to blame. One might want to explain the outrage and anger directed against Gorbachev and the authorities as defensive: a projection outwards of an unbearable hatred, unleashed by the helplessness central to the experience of disaster against the primary internal object for its failure to protect. It is plausible to think that this is exactly what the little girl in the group was expressing when she said, "All the children hate their fathers now"—perhaps hating father to keep mother good. Clinically, this may be what one takes up, but it should not blind us to the social–political dimension. For if all the children hate their fathers, there is a truth there, in that the fathers have let the children down; not because they did not stop the earthquake, but because they have not been in charge of their own destiny. The lesson Armenians are beginning to learn is that they cannot rely on anyone to protect them, certainly not the then Soviet Army or Gorbachev, and that if their children and women are not to be mutilated and killed again, they have to take up arms. I returned from Armenia with a heightened national consciousness, but also much more committed to psychoanalysis.

One of the rewards of going to a country where there is no psychoanalysis is discovering the power of psychoanalysis afresh. It is like being in the equivalent of Vienna, before Breuer and Freud (1895d), where instead of hysterics, people are bringing you children with a host of what to them seem incomprehensible symptoms and behaviours, and you can treat them as ordinary children suffering from reminiscences. It was amazing to discover the power of psychoanalytic concepts: conflict, guilt, anxiety, regression, identification with the aggressor, splitting, idealization, the work of mourning, and danger depicted in oral, anal, and genital phantasies. Again and again I would find myself interpreting the child's guilt at having survived dead siblings and friends; clinging to adults for safety while wanting to hit them for their failure to protect; feeling jealous of the dead sibling or father who claims all of mother's mind. With one particularly receptive boy we could in just two sessions formulate how, to quote him, "Good and bad are all mixed up in my mind", and how beneath his surface thoughts there is an oscillation between infantile omnipotence (he would have been able to save his cousin from under the rubble) and his infantile rage at the adults (they are responsible for the death of his cousin).

These are, of course, highlights, when something could be understood and put into words and one could sense relief from the child. Perhaps the relief was the greater because these children had little experience of anyone trying to understand them without controlling and constraining. Very withdrawn children in particular had been subjected to a lot of pressure—to talk, to play, to be cheered up—so one had to sit in silence and use countertransference and, with luck, pin something on a little piece of observation, like a girl's gaze being held by a set of hospital toys. The particular girl I have in mind had spent months lying with severe head injuries in a hospital abroad. Both of her parents were dead. She was living with her maternal aunt, while her brothers lived with paternal relatives in another town. She did not tell me any of this; she scarcely spoke at all. But there was a moment of communication. I had taken up how awkward it was for her to be sitting there with me, a stranger. She said, with a flicker of a resigned smile, that she was used to psychologists. We sat in silence. She then said, "But they left." I said she wished that they had not left and that she were at this moment with them rather than with me. She said, "What can I do? I have to fit in." This proved to be an exact formulation of her situation.

But above all it was the psychoanalytic stance itself: waiting and observing and listening, not rushing into questions, allowing for silence, listening to what was not said or observing what was not done. These—to us—absolutely ordinary things revealed themselves over there as most precious tools because, apart from enabling genuine if limited communication, they constituted for me the only stance adequate to and respectful of what these children had been through. Apart from the little bit of contact in the here-and-now, one had no idea where they were or what they felt. How could one know what they had experienced? How could they speak? Because any piece of telling involves hard work, as the session with A demonstrates.

When I was writing up the session with A, it had struck me that my crucial intervention had been to say that he would rather be with the others in the living-room and not in the kitchen with me. What had been understood and put into words was not just a here-and-now experience, but something very closely linked to the way that he, and he alone, had been trapped at the time of the earthquake in a room, unable to move. We can speculate that the understanding of his experience in the kitchen might have transformed his perception of me from a trapping and possibly also punishing object to a rescuing one. The point that I want to emphasize is this: once one has been trained to work in the transference, one seems naturally to scan the interaction for transference implications, though one may well choose not to articulate them.

Once A and I had pieced together his own story, we could see how he used the opportunity I gave him to voice questions of comparison—who else was trapped in his class?—which led him to tell me of the death of his classmate. I discovered when talking to adults in groups that they too found it hard to ask questions of one another and that the emotional climate changed once they could do so. This must be because in this area our motives cannot be entirely laudable: it is not just a question of "Was I the only one?" but also "Thank God I got off lightly compared to others." After all, who would be immune to the thought "Sooner him than me"? A went on to tell me the story about the boy who loved sweets, which, though possibly based on some bit of fact, had all the marks of phantasy about it. It plays with one of the major unconscious themes associated with disasters: disaster as punishment for sin. Also, there is a denial of the state of helplessness, the central experience during the moment of impact of a disaster, and particularly so in an earthquake that traps and immobilizes people—the boy in the larder was free to move about and did not even notice that an earthquake had taken place. He then switched round to a full acknowledgement of danger—he could have died—but only after he had shaped his narrative most elegantly to a humorous conclusion. One may see all sorts of defensive manoeuvres here, but for me at the time the main thing was that this boy, who had not been able to speak, was now playing with words and thoughts and that he was staging a play with me as his audience.

And here I want to refer again to Martha Wolfenstein (1957). Talking about the event, she says, enables a transformation of what is passive into what is active. The helpless victim becomes the effective story-teller, and the audience is made to undergo the experience. We are particularly alive to this aspect of communication in the present climate, with recent theoretical developments, especially Wilfred Bion's theory of the container and the contained. But Wolfenstein adds another, less current, thought: the orderliness of a narrative, she says, contrasts reassuringly with the inchoateness of the original experience. She emphasizes the active editing role of the narrator—the way that he or she may transform parts of the event, in a humorous way, for instance. It is an open question how much one respects the defensive aspects of the shaping of narrative in this sort of work. In a sense we may say that one of the things we do in long-term psychoanalytical work is to disallow a premature orderliness of narrative by analysing its defensive aspects. We have time, and we can allow for a greater reliving of inchoateness of experience—but not so in brief interventions, especially following a disaster.

Wolfenstein's thesis that the orderliness of a narrative has a therapeutic function in the mastery of trauma resonated to my own experience. Writing and addressing colleagues had become a crucial component in my own recuperation. Such thoughts led to a preoccupation with the theme of the function of narrative in recuperation from disaster. However, with time, as I listened to a large variety of narratives in Armenia, mostly from adults rather than children, I came to discriminate between those narratives that were in the service of recuperation and those that were not: repetitive set pieces, which were, rather, an expression of mental arrest. I came to the conclusion that it is not primarily the recounting of a story that is therapeutic, but the making of it and the kind of work that goes into this—for making involves grappling with chaos. Without some such work (which on the whole children were more able to engage in than adults), the story, while fulfilling the function of turning passive into active, is no more than self-proclamation. It may enable survival, but not the self-transformation implied in the word "therapeutic".

There was a different role I could take up with adults when I saw them in family settings. I could be a mediator between child and parent, facilitating the parents' understanding of the child. This was easier with some parents than with others, of course, depending upon the nature of their defences. A persistent issue was the adults' unwillingness to talk to their children about the death of close relatives. On my first visit, most people were hoping that the children would simply forget, thus sparing them the painful task, even though all the evidence pointed to the contrary. Many children were told that the absent sibling was abroad or in hospital. On my last trip, people were reluctantly coming to the conclusion that the children understood much more than they had supposed, and that they forgot nothing. In family interviews this was poignantly demonstrated in that it was often the child who introduced the subject of the dead sibling. With more receptive parents, those who were closer to being able to grasp their own pain and to withdraw the projection of not bearing to know from the child, it was possible to reach a point, in one interview, where they themselves would give me evidence that the child had known all along. For instance, one father said, in tears: "You're right, he doesn't believe that his sister is in the hospital. Every time we're near the cemetery he says to me: 'Dig Marena out of her grave.'"

Others were recalcitrant. I think of a woman, a paediatrician, who complained about the extreme aggressiveness of one of her two sons. During the second interview, the object of complaint had shifted to the quiet child. Eventually, we reached the subject of her dead husband, and her complaint became that while one child talked about his father incessantly, the other one scarcely mentioned him in her presence, though he would to others. She felt pestered by one and rejected by the other. When I commented on how she was talking to me in hushed tones, she said that she had never talked to the children about their father's death. She acknowledged that they knew anyway, but added: "They don't know it finally." When I said how hard it must be for her, as well, to know it finally, she gave me the impression of literally not having heard me. She went on to comment in a bitter tone: "Look how well they play together." Earlier she had said that they fought an awful lot and that they scarcely ever played together. I often noticed that some of the children were visibly freed and got on with their play when a parent could use me to talk about their own difficulties. It was worrying to see that this process, benign in itself, acted as a further irritant for this mother. She did not return for the third appointment.

To my initial tentative conclusion that the children were often bearing a double burden—their own and that of the adults—I would now add the following thoughts. First, their own conflicts are overwhelming and incomprehensible to them. Second, the help they need from adults is not available because of the adults' own mental state. But thirdly, and more destructively, they are the recipients of the adults' projections.

There is also the projection of hope into the children. The children represent the survival of the nation. This is inevitable after all disasters of vast proportions, but it has an added dimension in Armenia, given the political situation. There is nothing wrong with this, except that, if you are the incarnation of national continuity, you are not allowed to be weak or disturbed: you must be strong, cheerful, learn well at school, must draw nice pictures, and sing nationalist songs.

And what if you are an adult and have decided that there is nothing to be said for being a victim of massacres, you have to stand up and fight? And if you are fighting at the borders, or know that your security depends on those of your compatriots who are fighting, how much fighting for inner truth, how much suspension of narrative closure can you afford to go in for? This is one set of questions with which I end.

The other has to do with the subject of corruption and the difficulties of psychoanalytic practice within a totalitarian society. The earthquake relief organization to which I am attached planned to facilitate the creation of local centres and to offer support and training to newly recruited local workers. This was my task on my last visit. The problems were colossal. In the town in which I work, you could not activate the social structures without having the First Secretary of the Communist Party on your side. Gradually, I discovered that this man's promises meant nothing, not even when they were written on pieces of paper with lots of seals. I felt on my own skin what the bereaved people were talking about when they said that even to get what was officially their due, they had to spend hours, days, months queuing at party offices, pestering and pleading with officials, which means a mixture of servility and carefully judged histrionics. I say nothing of money passing hands. This is not only distressing, it is also dysfunctional, especially if time is limited and instead of training staff you find yourself negotiating with Comrade X, the First Secretary, in order to ensure that the huts promised to your psychological centre are at least connected to the mains water supply. And it is more than the water supply that this man controls. It is an open secret at the hospital that the Chief Physician is his appointee. Also, any doctor who is invited to train abroad must have Comrade X's approval to get a visa.

There are many like Comrade X, some bearing party cards, others who have opportunistically discarded their cards and made a virtue of it. It is a nightmare when one is trying to get anything done outside the consulting-room, which, even without water and electricity, came to feel like a haven because outside it one did not know whom to trust.

So, what am I doing, when, in response to my observation of staff conflicts I observe in a psychological centre that has barely started functioning, I say that they should institute weekly staff discussions in order to attempt to talk to one another openly? I have to remind myself that these people have grown up in a society where truthfulness and trustfulness, far from not getting you connected to the water supply, have often, until recently, led to exile or death.

It is a cause for celebration that in the first free elections the Armenian people elected a decent government. They now have a parliament rather like that of Czechoslovakia or Lithuania. Some say the days of Comrade X are limited, but I do not know. How long does it take to change the emotional legacy of culture? Psychoanalysts in the West take for granted a social milieu where it is safe to speak out in public, which could, in Armenia, until relatively recently, lead to exile or death. What kind of home psychoanalysis can find in such conditions is an open question.

CHAPTER EIGHT

On losing your marble

Alasdair Honeyman

Experte credite
Trust one who has gone through it

Virgil, *Aeneid*, xi.283

Joseph had a bone tumour in his hip called an osteosarcoma. Because of its position, it had time to grow quite large before it came to anyone's attention. This is an excerpt from Joseph's life, when he was on the ward where I worked for eight months. It is also the story of how we got to know each other, and how we negotiated the reality of his osteosarcoma, whose various guises you will get to know.

Joseph's marble was as big as an orange. He was eight when he arrived on the ward with his parents, and the diagnosis truly stove in on them like a wave. Questions whirled and spumed, but with neither easy answers nor easy solutions, it was difficult to know what words to offer. What armbands, what dinghy, what raft could help? This was their hurricane of disorientation. It was Joseph's marble, Joseph's malignancy, Joseph's nasty thing growing in his hip as big as an orange. How could I sit tight with this blast of knowledge as they flailed about in its wake?

There are similarities with falling into the Baltic Sea. The sea is cold, getting out of it is a struggle, and it has to be achieved quickly if you want to survive. As a rescuer, can I truly insulate myself and speed about inflatable-like on the surface, or am I going to be in the water too? In any event, the plan is to hook Joseph out of the water quickly and safely.

The thread that is Joseph's new life on the oncology ward, which has become his lifeline, is a white, double-lumened Hickman or chemotherapy line, through which we can safely give powerful drugs. It is his new umbilical cord, except that this one disappears into his chest and will be attached to him until the end of his treatment. This is the heart of the matter. He is now on board a ship larger than he can imagine. We in the medical profession trust and believe that it is a fine ship that can bite the waves, that he and his family having been picked up, they will be glided out of those Baltic depths, past the head of the Jutland peninsula, and off back to home and to a normal life on terra firma. We make haste, and in their shocked and cold-bitten state, it is enough that they hold onto the guide-rails and enquire what the halyards are, how the sheets work, and what holds up the mast.

In the privacy of his mother-tongue Joseph expresses his feelings vociferously to his parents. We can but imagine what is being said. Why this trip? Where are they taking him? Who are all these people? What is this ship, this drip, this blood test, this investigation, this Hickman line, this pain, this chemotherapy, and when is this tide of vomiting going to end?

The ship sails on, and to begin with Joseph is well enough to walk around with his drip stand and the chemotherapy hanging on it. It is not much to be attached to. He did not choose it. It is cold and sterile. He cannot cuddle it at night, and it cannot comfort him when he feels low and he cannot discard it. Fortunately he has found the playroom and the Lego. He has been making the most wonderful models of planes and space ships, and we all marvel at his imagination and his quick-spiritedness. He has also been drawing and making volcanoes, great orange and yellow and red masterpieces of papier mâché. He has a lot to blow his top about.

There are three or so separate weeks of chemotherapy before Joseph's anticipated surgery. By the third admission, I feel that I am beginning to make some headway with the family, and they with me. The formalities of a doctor–patient relationship can become a hindrance, and it is not always easy to break through them. When Joseph's father comments on my severe haircut, suggesting that it does not appear to have helped to improve my intelligence quotient, it is a welcome blow to my super-hero, super-understanding status. It gives me a chance to have a more straightforward and genuine relationship. I feel grateful to him, albeit surprised by the way he has made contact with me. I feel foolish, and I wonder why, and whether it is good or bad.

There is a clown at the Christmas party with whom I identify profoundly. He has the pace and the rhythm of those about him, including me. Behind his immaculate and hideous mask and the tumble of apparent surprises, the children can intimately see him and his tragedy. They identify with his swanking about in his comfortably and colourfully edged white coat and his gigantic shoes. They have to work out his tricks for him, and his delights they have anticipated before he appears to have realized them himself. Folly and madness interplay gently, and we can all safely enjoy it. Joseph is free of his drip stand today and follows the clown about closely, accomplice-like. The joking, playing, and mucking about bring him delight, and it is wonderful to see him this way. This is the calm before the next very adult journey that he is going to take.

Joseph's operation, like everything else that happened to him in the preceding months, is very big. He has had more scans, which show that there are no metastases (spread to anywhere else in the body), so Mr Quorn the surgeon is going to chop it out. After the operation, and four days of intensive care, Joseph is back on the ward. He looks exhausted and he is not able to do much. He is on a special mattress that sings quietly all the time as it rests him on a six-inch bed of air. It is a mournful place for Joseph to be, and people recognize his need for quiet and for gentle care and handling. It is difficult to know yet how to make contact with him, or whether to just let him be. After a week, something happens. He has started to play with the Lego again, and he has begun to look out from his bed to watch the comings and goings of all the people about the nurses' station opposite him. Perhaps he is ready to join in again, perhaps also to draw more volcanoes. He looks intermittently furious as well as fed-up, bored, frustrated, and irritable. And he is stuck in bed.

One afternoon, Joseph's grandmother is with him. We chat about his plight, and, in hearing distance of Joseph, I suggest my concerns about his losing his marbles. Grandma concurs immediately. Joseph does not look up. We talk on about how we might recover them. Grandma is smiling, and this friendly banter makes me feel good. I wonder how I might extend this marble-losing story to include Joseph himself. There are some real marbles in the playroom, and together with a colleague we contrive to hide them in Joseph's bed. With able distraction from grandma, it is difficult to know how much Joseph is caring to take in and how much he has not noticed. We do eventually "find" the marbles, and Joseph looks delighted in a protesting way, especially when we decide to use his toes as a suitable conduit to prevent their future loss. In fact, one of the marbles does go missing, and we have to leave Joseph and his grandma to find it on their own.

By the next day, the marble has been found, I have my comeuppance, and Joseph has his moment. He shouts out as we are starting the ward round that he has found the marble, and he holds it out to me. With deft timing, as he gives it back, he explains that it is in fact my marble and that I have only one.

Joseph's story does not include the technicalities of the medicine, nor the supporting underlay of basic science. The latter is immense and powerful, and it continues to grow. And it is these domains that primarily constitute the scaffolding from which doctors work. It is also a business, and in the name of competence and efficiency the need to be busy is enormous, as is the turnover of patients. The bottom line is that they are treated and that the care is satisfactory. The structure of the organization and the working relationships within it are driven by this. The social anthropologists would have a field day delineating the typology of these interactions.

Somewhere in this hive of activity sits the punter, the patient, the human being whose disorder is to have a body that does not work, either as it should or as he or she would like it to. To some of these people I am no more than a contract cleaner. I examine their broken arm, I request an X-ray of it, I arrange treatment and follow-up. There is no loss in the continuity in their lives, and the relationship we have is not so different from that between a shopper and a checkout desk. I see them fleetingly, and our respective behaviour is immaterial to the outcome. This is the straightforward, technical end of the work that in your training you learn mostly through practice, just like riding a bike. Each patient is but part of a continuity of disease whose language you learn to speak and think. A goal in training is for this language to become second nature. The primary aesthetic satisfaction is in its mastery.

Anaesthesia can, however, arise, particularly with the same puzzle being pieced together time and time again. There is a varying configuration of pieces: number, shape, size, hue, but the picture is the same. The next one to see is another asthmatic or another headache or another abdo pain. Casualty and the punters become boring because the work can be predictable and mundane. Even the real emergencies can stop being exciting because you know what to do. The obvious place of refuge from this ennui is in greater technicality: the double-sided puzzle with one thousand pieces just of cherries on stalks, demanding the tireless picking and packaging of a whole crop of busy doctors.

This paradigm of work in medicine is not the only one, but it is incessant and obvious to those who regard it from outside, particularly and ironically and increasingly so from the punters at the receiving end, for whom it matters a great deal how they are treated. The gaze upon them is the disinterested clinical domain, where the signifier, the symptom, the night-time cough, and the wheeze already signify the disease asthma. This weaving together is the ultimate strength in the medicine of the last two hundred years and perhaps the origin of our pathological view of our inside and outside world, which can appear all too tidily wrapped up.

In paediatrics, it is less easy to avoid the palavers of a stricken child than that of a well-behaved adult. The parents are also acutely sensitive to the vulnerability of their offspring, and they are keen to know that you are taking all of their plight seriously. And who is to guess what consequences there will be following my actions in one of those acute moments? If I should happen to be rough when I am taking blood and I lie about it not hurting, does that mean the child is going to be needle-phobic for the rest of the treatment for their brain tumour? If I provide another few minutes in casualty listening to a parent's anxiety about their child's treatment, does that mean that the child's asthma will be better controlled because the child will be receiving his or her medicine? It sounds so obvious, but in the heat of the moment, unless I am able to walk around with that third ear truly open, how can I be expected to manage the disease and the patient together? Where do I get the support or the supervision or the training to do that? Who knows what I might end up hearing, seeing, or feeling?

While still at college, in a gesture of enormous frustration, I suggested to a consultant friend of mine that I might wait until I was 50 years old before I started work, because that way I might just have enough experience of life and human nature to be able to bear the suffering that I was sure to see and then respond to it without sounding too silly. His retort was that I should not worry, because I was sure to be 50 within a couple of years. What is missed in this leap into middle to late-middle age is the opportunity to joke and play and muck about, to grow up, to be messy, to not know, to be frightened, to fall off your bike and eat the cherries—things that medical students try to squeeze in between adolescence and turning up on the wards presentable and ready to perform the paraphernalia of everyday medical duties, not having touched a breast or a penis, let alone examined one, not knowing about death, or divorce, or violence, or suffering, or rottenness other than vicariously. Being youthful and intelligent and resilient, they can gainfully and ably work out what they need to perform to get through the course without realizing what is happening to them. They have little experience in asking who they want to be other than the title that they are striving for. And there are few who want or care to know.

Unaware of its epistemology, we find it comforting to believe in a tidy predetermined path that the origins and methods of medical knowledge have supposedly followed. Such was not the case, nor will it be in the future. Enveloped in its well-worn mantle, we can feel safe in the way we practise medicine. In each flurry of medical activity, through our knowledge and skill we can re-enact and display our having conquered our fears and anxieties of not knowing. However, in contradistinction, outside their small sphere, doctors, just like others, do say silly things about human nature. And despite this they have yet to embrace the psychological insights that are available to them.

With Winnicott comes the first generous attempt to engage from within with the classical medical model and the youthful, stroppy, adolescent paradigms that were nested by Freud and his colleagues at the beginning of this century. It was a courageous step. Winnicott was not well liked by his contemporaries in paediatrics. They must have hated him. There is anxiety enough in one paradigm meeting its own boundaries, let alone two—medicine and psychology—meeting face to face; and any craft that tries to navigate between them risks forfeiting its rights to either. Winnicott, Argonaut-like, took the risk, and he showed that the journey was possible. His ambition and passion invite us to travel the same route, despite its dangers.

So what of the next generation of psychologically aware paediatricians? Is such a combination still possible? Certainly, I believe the profession is crying out for them. But there are a few pioneers yet who still need to map out the ecology of the inner world of paediatricians and of paediatrics—a foundation of mental health of its practitioners and patients. Their contribution is to risk facing their own anxiety of not knowing, of experiencing new territory, the folly of getting lost, and the mockery and fear and jealousy of those they leave behind and those to whom they return. Sentimental it will not be.

If Winnicott were alive and with us now, do you imagine he would trust us to carry on his work? I imagine that he would invite us to climb down into the thick of it, that he would stay near enough for us to know he was about, that he would show us how to mend punctures and pick up the cherry stones, and if we mislaid any of your marbles, then he would help us to look for them.

CHAPTER NINE

The false self and the false body

Susie Orbach

This collection of essays gives me an opportunity both to pay tribute to Winnicott, from whom we have all learned so much, and also to clarify and extend one of his most famous concepts—that of the "false self". I believe that this central concept of Winnicott's has been misunderstood, that the adaptive and creative aspects of the false self as a response to an unfacilitating environment has not been sufficiently appreciated, and that once we understand Winnicott's metaphor more fully, the way will open to extend this powerful concept to include the concept of a "false body". The extension of the false self to include a false body illuminates current difficulties in our understanding of psychosomatic development, as well as opening up the analyst's bodily experiences as an important but often neglected dimension of clinical work.

As I begin to write, I am aware of my desire to surrender to the sensuousness of Winnicott's idiom, to be held by his concepts and to allow my thinking and writing to come from that place that he calls the transitional experience. The atmosphere he creates in his psychoanalytic writing combines an understanding of the profound and the highly personal. He makes, for the reader, a facilitating environment, out of which the personal means for creativity can flourish.

Winnicott's project addressed the essence of what it is to be human. He had a magnificent sense of human possibility. In his sensitive, thoughtful, intelligent, and—one might almost say—sensual technical writing, he touches and transforms our understanding of human consciousness and agency in both a mental and a physical sense, curling into mental spaces that had previously lain undescribed. He struggles to find the language that can describe that which gives, or fails to give, meaning to an individual's life and experience of selfhood.

His writing strives to articulate what Christopher Bollas (1987), a contemporary interpreter of his work, has termed, in his own work, "the unthought known". Winnicott enters into that which has not yet been formulated but is experienced. It is in the process of giving form to experience that transformation occurs and our understanding of human behaviour, human desire, and human motivation is enhanced.

The sensuality of Winnicott's writing expresses his attempt to enter into the lived experience of the analysand and the analyst, the baby and the mother, and the parents. His is a relational theory, a theory that recognizes that the uniqueness of the individual is inextricably and intimately linked with the relationships within which it is formed. It is Winnicott who wrote that "there is no such thing as a baby". His theories, his understanding of psychological development, his clinical innovations, and his numerous concepts, such as the transitional object, the false self, the use of the object, the good-enough mother, have all entered the psychoanalytic canon. Their widespread application, the way in which they can be meaningfully stretched to accommodate new understandings, speaks to the depth of understanding Winnicott achieved of the human subject.

Two quotations from Winnicott settle upon me many days when I am with a patient whose hurt seems unbearable, or when I am writing, and trying to make sense of my experience as a psychotherapist, parent, patient, friend, lover. They form a theoretical cradle holding an understanding of what happens when things go wrong in early life. The quotations dignify what might in a colder hand be mere clinical descriptions of the psychic structure. In Winnicott's writings, they illustrate with grace the dilemmas at the heart of human subjectivity.

The first quotation talks about a phenomenon that is often observed and often felt in the countertransference. The analysand is unable to experience himself or herself as being viable, worthy, and as existing for her or himself in a reliable way. Winnicott discusses the way a troubled, fragmented person may constitute a sense of being for herself or himself by generating emergencies, or moments of intensity, which by their very nature require attention and solutions. In the establishment of such *crises*, the person gathers up for herself or himself a sense that he or she engenders, manages, and does: therefore he or she is. As Winnicott wrote:

> Survival is sought in the management of crises. In other words the person has no real sense of continuity of being an ongoing proposition themselves. They provide this continuity for themselves through the creation, management and survival of crises . . . in extreme cases the infant exists only on the basis of a continuity of reactions to impingement and recoveries from such reactions. [Winnicott, 1965]

For Winnicott, this problem—the lack of continuity or belief in self—arises when the infant's uniqueness has not been able to be recognized. It has instead been negated. But instead of giving up, of turning away from the possibility of relationship, of collapsing into psychic annihilation, the infant finds and develops aspects of the self that can capture and hold the interest of the caregiver:

> The mother who is not good enough is not able to implement the infant's omnipotence, and so she repeatedly fails to meet the infant gesture; instead she substitutes her own gesture which is to be given sense by the compliance of the infant. This compliance on the part of the infant is the earliest stages of the False Self, and belongs to the mother's inability to sense her infant's needs. [Winnicott, 1960c, p. 145]

This second quotation, addressing the aetiology of the false self in earliest experience, shows Winnicott finding a language that describes pre-linguistic emotional transactions. The shape of the relationship in which these interactions occur is shaped by the mother's psychology and by the child's creative adaptation to what it is offered. In its adaptation to the maternal substitution of her gesture for the infant's gesture, the infant begins to develop a false self *as an expression of personal agency,* as an active adaptation to an otherwise unworkable situation. Humans work with possibilities—possibilities that can be recognized within the relational field. That which is not recognized cannot quite exist. But the resilience and adaptability of the human infant is such that it will search for those aspects of self that *can* receive validation. It will live then with the tension of wanting to bring forth the unrecognized aspects of self (Winnicott's true self), while not being able to trust that they are of value.

This complicated idea of Winnicott's can easily be misconstrued. A common reading renders the false self as simply the protector of the true self unable to activate itself. But I believe Winnicott was getting at more than this. I think he is telling us about the way in which subjectivity or subjectivities are formed in the relational field and the textural and feeling tones of the different self states humans can encompass. His idea that what the child offers back to the caregiver when its first gestures have been nullified, while it is adaptive and false, is nevertheless real and demonstrates the complexity of human subjectivity. The false self is no less real than the true self. Or, to put it another way, the defence structure is an aspect of the self. It contains inclinations, ways of being that need to be linked with the less developed, less visible, less recognized aspects of the self (the true self).

The false self has been constructed within a relationship. Winnicott tells us that its aetiology lies in the infant's acceptance of the mother's gestures. The infant confirms the mother through entering into her gesture and making it theirs—both the mother's and the baby's. The false self is a practised self, in that the person has used it for self expression. The true self contains possibilities, hidden aspects of the personality that are feared and dreaded. The psychoanalytic therapeutic relationship is a place for the true self possibilities and fears to emerge, for its gestures to be recognized and engaged with. The true self, like the false self, grows in the context of a relationship.

The false self and the true self need to come to a different accommodation with one another. In that new accommodation there can be an integration of those aspects of the person that have been forged defensively, and those that are as yet undeveloped. If we see the false self in this way—as a real self in its own right rather than as a temporary keeper of the real person—we can understand that psychic structural change needs to incorporate these aspects of self rather than jettison them. That which has been developed "falsely" is of value and cannot simply be given up or lost.

Many patients seek psychotherapy and psychoanalysis because of a felt disjuncture between their different selves. The private self is often a self who feels shame. The public self, or the one that keeps them going, is a self whose nourishment depends upon a short-term fix. Deconstructing the content, the feelings, the purposes, derivations of these different aspects of self minimizes the space between the true self and the false self. Where a hole existed between these two self-conceptions, which neither filled, their association makes it possible for the person to integrate and turn *outside in* those attributes that were once felt simply to hang on the surface of the person and to turn *inside out* those that were once hidden and deeply private. The interpenetration of these aspects of the self— the defensive false self and the private true self—now permeate the psychic structure, giving it strength, resilience, and the capacity to grow, to be nourished, and to nourish.

Winnicott did not propose a new term for the accommodation of the false self and the true self. He tried to flesh out what were felt as distinctive self states that in the course of a therapy could come to a less troublesome state of being. His attention to these senses of self (senses of self that I imagine were articulated by his patients), shows us his respect for the patient's experiences as well as his profound capacity for understanding early psychic development. His therapeutic work is not about the substitution of one state for another but about the knitting together of the adapted self (the false self) with a true self of possibilities that now out of hiding has a chance to develop (cf. Davies & Frawley, 1994).

Winnicott's work on the true self and the false self has been particularly useful to me in trying to push current analytic practice with adults beyond what I have come to describe as its "mentalist period" (Orbach, 1995). Freud's work laid the foundations for a science of body and mind. Indeed, Breuer and Freud's (1895d) work on hysteria was among the very first to establish the connections between certain physical symptomatology and emotional life.

Although the early period of psychoanalysis is marked by a high degree of interest in the interrelatedness of psyche and soma, this aspect of psychoanalysis—with notable exceptions—has not been in ascendancy during the post–World-War-II period. While work with children necessitates explicit attention to a child's physicality, it has been quite possible within adult psychoanalysis to disregard the body unless it inserts itself in especially powerful ways in the consulting-room (cf. Davies & Frawley, 1994; Sinason, 1992).

Present discussion of psychosomatic or hysterical symptomatology has tended to privilege discourse about the psychic, seeing physical symptoms as manifestations of psychic distress rather than as indicators of disturbance in the psychosomatic development of the individual. Furthermore, within a mentalist psychoanalysis, physical actions taken by the individual—such as, for instance, the cutting of self, the wish of the transsexual to remove external genitalia, the stuffing and purging of the body in bulimia and anorexia—are explained in terms of their psychic functions. They are classed as derivatives of psychic disturbance without due reference to the psychosomatic field in which the human being's body develops. This is often the case even in sexual abuse or physical abuse situations where the patient's body has been penetrated or violated literally but the therapist's preoccupation is with a mental penetration and violation. The vulnerability of the body is translated as an emotional vulnerability (which, of course, it is), but the physical basis of that vulnerability is rarely addressed. Winnicott's work both on the aetiology of the false self and on the mind and its relation to the psyche–soma provide the basis for a paradigm shift, for reintegrating that which has become inaccurately and falsely separated into distinct but unviable discrete entities of body and mind (Winnicott, 1954).

I have found it particularly useful to extend Winnicott's work on the false self to the notion of the false body. I suggest that the individual's corporeality reflects not only instability in emotional development but instability and a lack of recognition in physical, somatic development as well. In other words, we must go further than to see the body as the recipient or container of psychic distress (Bick, 1968; McDougall, 1989; Pines, 1980) and, instead, to problematize a false body that is allied to the false self (Orbach, 1986, 1994, 1995). The body and the mind are coparticipants in the psychosomatic drama. The false body can be understood as a parallel development to the false self: the gestures of the parental body overwhelm the gestures of the infant's body. Furthermore, if the parental body is itself a false body, this will be internalized and complied with, so that the mother and child are connected by false bodies. There is, of course, a related and complex issue: the internalization of the parental false self and false body and its role in the genesis of the baby's false sense of self.

In extending Winnicott's ideas about the self to the body, it is, then, possible to link in with those observations of Margaret Mahler and her colleagues who, in writing of children who have not been able to achieve physical or emotional separation from their mothers, have bodies that are analogous to Winnicott's false selves—bodies that fail to be fully alive for the person (Mahler, Pine, & Bergman, 1975). They are, rather, inanimate or predifferentiated. Mahler's ideas on the psychological birth of the infant correlate with problems at the level of physical existence: problems in the physical embeddedness of the individual or what Winnicott (1971c, p. 8) calls "psychosomatic indwelling".

Such a shift into thinking of the body as a coparticipant in the drama of the development of the self, rather than the bit player (dustbin?) that carries that which is inconvenient and psychically uncontainable, is of considerable value in clinical work. It helps us understand and approach phenomena that are often elusive. It also suggests modifications in technique.

In wanting to suggest some technical innovations, I run into a paradox of highlighting the body at the same time as I am arguing that the body needs to be thought of not as separate from but as a central part of the psyche–soma self. This is a conundrum because of our current mentalist preoccupations. But I am highlighting our relationship to the body in order to begin the process of integrating and reintegrating the corporeal with the psychic.

A useful tool for accomplishing this integration is to regard the countertransference as a possible bit of information about the construction of the patient's body, just as we do for information about the construction of the patient's psyche. This means observing and registering the physical, the palpably corporeal responses that are aroused in the clinical situation. At the technical level, it means extending our view of the countertransference beyond the registering of emotional affects and the enactment of role-responsiveness (Sandler, 1976) or reciprocal role (Ryle, 1990), to observe the physical dimensions of our experience that occur during the course of our work.

I want to give a few brief examples of what I mean. In employing the notion of false body over the last decade, I have found three particular ways in which it might announce itself in the psychotherapy relationship.

1.   There can be a felt request or demand within the countertransference for physical provision. I have written elsewhere of the bodily states that have been evoked in the countertransference, notably the evocation of a contented, purring body in the psychotherapist as an external body for use by a patient who had a hated body (Orbach, 1995). This body was understood by the psychotherapist as a creation on the part of the patient who needed a stable body in the room from which to deconstruct her hated "true body" and thus begin the process of developing a body that contained rather than split her ambivalence about her physical existence.

The evocation of bodily arousal in another way has been reported to me by a psychotherapist who experienced stimulation of the "let-down reflex"—the reflex that nursing mothers feel when their babies are ready to feed—during the treatment of a regressed patient. This therapist, who had not breast-fed for 15 years, felt the tingling of the let-down reflex over an extended period of three-times-weekly psychotherapy. The therapist noted these physical feelings in herself as well as more specific feelings around feeding and being fed from. She had the sense of being sucked at in differing ways, sometimes contentedly, sometimes hurriedly, sometimes anxiously, sometimes angrily. These countertransference responses were discussed with the patient for their physical and psychological meanings.

2.   Using the idea of the false body, one has a way to engage with the bringing of physical distress into the therapy relationship, where it can be admitted, explored, and—through the acceptance of it by the psychotherapist—integrated into the body of the person. What had previously remained hidden and unexplored found shape in the psychotherapeutic relationship and could then saturate the physical and psychological experience of the person.

An easily understood example of this involves a woman of 35 years of age, who moved her chair and body so closely into the space of the therapist that the therapist found herself moving her chair back. The patient then inched her chair closer, and the therapist observed this time her desire to move away again, to create a physical space between them that felt comfortable. The chair-moving ensued over several sessions. The therapist felt crowded out and gagged. She felt nauseous, and as if she were being physically overtaken. In trying to understand her response to the patient and the physical ambience between them, she reflected on what she knew of the physical handling of the patient in infancy. The patient had sicked up frequently in early childhood and then bed-wetted. The patient remembers being scolded for bed-wetting and so then graduated to migraine and vomiting.

The patient and psychotherapist understood together many of the symbolic meanings of the bed-wetting, migraine, and vomiting, but it was the therapist's attention to the use of the interpersonal physical space in the room that brought directly into the treatment the patient's difficulties with indwelling and accepting her body. The therapist suggested at one point that the patient's body was to some extent unplotted for the patient. She did not know where it began and ended, and that it was only in its encounter with an other, with its butting up against another, that her own physicality could be experienced. The body ego was invaded, not bounded, and the patient searched for a physical boundary in relation to another so that she could make that boundary her own.

In this instance, we could begin to make sense of this patient's difficulties with her body. The spontaneous gestures of the true body, the sicking-up, were not received in a natural sense or as a message about too much milk going in at one time. They were, instead, translated into rejection of the mother. The daughter took on this idea, and she gave compliance to her mother's gesture as her own. Her physical responses then embodied both her own gesture and that of her mother's reading of them. The true body fought for a presence through the migraine, the vomiting, the encroachment on the space of another. In the psychotherapy, the distress that attached to the rejected aspects of the body was received. The therapist saw her experience as an attempt on the part of the patient to be physically recognized. That the patient was pushy and evoked a desire on the part of the therapist to move away was a hint about the body instability and the anxiety about physical connection. The therapist's understanding of this led the way for the transformation of physical discomfort, disease, and the emergence of a body within the therapy relationship that was both bounded and connected.

3. Another way in which I have observed the false body coming to therapy is where the therapist experiences in the countertransference a version of the physical distress the patient experiences. I have written elsewhere about the countertransference feelings of disintegration and disassembling (Orbach, 1995) conveyed from supervisee to supervisor in the case of a patient whose physical sense of self was so precarious that she needed to confirm her physicality by cutting herself. The supervisee and the supervisor in discussing the case both seemed to float off.

Since I reported this, many psychotherapists have told me of the struggles they have experienced in trying to stay awake with a particular patient. The physical demand in the countertransference is for sleep. Of course, there can be no single understanding of such a phenomenon aroused in the therapist. The inducement to sleep can have as many meanings as patients, and can vary its meaning in the course of a treatment. The sleep could be a request for the capacity to be alone in the presence of another (Winnicott, 1958b). The sleep could be a request to integrate the physical and the psychological. The sleep could also be a search for shared soothing, and so on. The variety of therapists' experiences and responses points to the value in extending Winnicott's idea of the false self to the body. When we extend the concept, we can explore, rather than reduce to the symbolic, the physical aspects of enactments in the therapy or the countertransference.

If the false self is created in relation to the mother's or caregiver's psychology, then the false body is similarly a relational construct. The possibility of a true body cannot emerge until there is a relationship to receive it. We can receive the true body and deconstruct the false body if we tune ourselves to the more physical aspects of the interpersonal exchange. As Freud tells us, we need to tune our unconscious like a radio receiver to the unconscious of the other in order to receive their signals. Our work can benefit by extending this metaphor in a physical sense, by tuning our bodies so that we can receive signals at a physical level in response to a particular patient. We can observe what is aroused in us physically, how we place ourselves, whether we feel physically at ease, or in discomfort, and so on.

Attention to such details enables us to extend Winnicott's work into domains about which he was implicit rather than explicit. In being explicit, we begin to dissolve the divide not just between the true self and the false self but also between the "body self" and the "mental self".

PART FOUR

REMINISCENCES OF WINNICOTT

CHAPTER TEN

Memories of Donald Winnicott

E. James Anthony

I am quite delighted about this book for Donald Winnicott, and I am sure that he will be pleased. He reacted with pain when he felt that his contributions were overlooked or seized upon and quoted without acknowledgement, although he was ready to admit that he himself was never sure from where at least a few of his plethora of ideas originated. However, his paradoxical, meta-psychic, eccentric expressive talents were all inimitably his own, and they gave his work a recognizable stamp that immediately differentiated his thinking from that of other British psychoanalysts—except perhaps Marion Milner (1972, 1978), whose wonderful caricatured portrayal of him stays forever in my mind.

I will select a few memories of him that stick out in my mind. He was the chairman of the examining board of the Institute of Psycho-Analysis in London that assembled to assess my competence to become a member. My membership paper was accepted and my answers to questions apparently passed muster, but what I recall very distinctly was his encouraging smile and his repeated efforts to set me—a nervous "me"—at ease. I also remember clinging to a piece of paper containing what I thought to be crucial concepts until it was soaked with sweat, and I imagined wondering whether he perceived me with his remarkably observant eyes as clinging for dear life to my transitional object!

After I reviewed his *Collected Papers: Through Paediatrics to Psycho-Analysis* (Winnicott, 1958a) most favourably, DW wrote to me in America, where I had settled, to say with his usual buoyancy that my critique had given his ego a much-needed boost, for which he was very grateful. He hoped that I was adjusting well to the new and "strange" environment. After all these years, the chapters that come to mind were all part of his humanness: falling asleep during a session, hating the little boy who gave him so much trouble, getting rid of the child—a control case—who bit him twice in the buttock, and about whom he remarked with some feeling that he should never have been in analysis, but under firmer management. It is interesting how this managerial approach has caught on with all those long-suffering clinicians dealing with antisocial children.

I remember referring a little girl to him transatlantically, and I also remember his careful and very intuitive evaluation of her. For reasons that seemed just right, he suggested that she should be treated by Barbara Dockar-Drysdale at the Mulberry Bush School outside Oxford, mentioning that in this way he could keep a watchful eye on her progress, since he saw Mrs Dockar-Drysdale on a regular supervisory basis and he thought highly of her therapeutic abilities. I thought of her, as I was acquainted with her at the Maudsley Hospital, as empathically immersed in him and in the patients whom she saw, and I was glad to follow through with his recommendation. Here, I thought to myself, was a paediatrician who appraised a disturbed child with all the combined skills of a child psychiatrist and child psychoanalyst. Even when I was in London, he had suggested that you did not need a training in child psychiatry (contradicting Sir Aubrey Lewis) before treating child psychiatric cases: any analysed paediatrician could do it.

When he agreed, after much coaxing, to participate in a book on *Parenthood: Its Psychology and Psychopathology*, put together by Therese Benedek and myself (Anthony & Benedek, 1970), he was slow to send in his chapter, and it required some pressure on my part eventually to elicit his manuscript. We had discussed what he might write, but it still surprised me when it finally came. It was exceedingly Winnicottian and had to do with "let-down" babies—

a woman who had failed in a six-year analysis (Winnicott, 1970). What a challenge to DW! One associated this immediately with Sándor Ferenczi's "nursery" technique—especially when a mutual "rocking" takes place with Winnicott as analyst, which he refers to as the early stages of baby care. Both Ferenczi and DW were *enfants terribles* to their colleagues, and both had attractive and appealing personalities. Both dedicated themselves to the care of traumatized small or big persons, and both were very conscious of the horrors of overwhelming impingements.

In the volume that I edited with George Pollock, *Parental Influences in Sickness and in Health* (Anthony & Pollock, 1985), I wrote the Introduction, although Pollock's name was included in the listing, and reviewed Winnicott's thoughts, as a childless person, from pages 5 to 10, comparing his ideas to those of Anna Freud, also a childless person. I enjoyed his comment, so tilted in his own direction, that the father represented "the liveliness of the street" and mother "the stability of the home". But he always denied that he was sentimental about mothers, and he referred to their love as "a pretty crude affair". I also like his view that parents need children in order to become better spouses.

My last personal contact with him took place in Rome, when we had both been invited to address the psychoanalytic society there. When we were not doing this, we walked the streets of the old city with Clare, just talking about the oldness of surrounding things, and I assumed that he was feeling his oldness, which showed in our slow pace of progress. Clare was lovingly managerial. When he arrived for the meeting, he elected to speak second, and my agreement to this was a huge mistake on my part. I gave an abstruse theoretical paper in a language not understood by the majority present, and communication must have been near to zero. I know I was confronted by blank faces and eyes politely kept open. The second presentation was a huge success, engaged the audience, and provoked them to a stimulating discussion. What DW did was to present slides with squiggles that spoke for themselves, and he used a minimum of speech, a good deal of non-verbal communication, and much affective expression, and he had the analysts eating out of his hand. I felt hot with embarrassment and full of envy. This man knew how to get across to people, how to conduct play therapy with foreign adults ready to regress in the service of the ego, especially after they had been suffocated by an overdose of turgid secondary process.

I never saw DW again, but I continued to love the shape of his mind, and I teach, with pleasure, his ways to candidates at our Institute, making use of a similar playfulness.

CHAPTER ELEVEN

My experience of Winnicott

Hugh Gee

Oxford

My tutor in psychology specialized in perception, and his tolerance of Freud and the dynamic branch of psychology was almost non-existent. At that time, I was unaware of the differences that existed within the field of psychology, and my own inclinations towards psychoanalytical concepts were treated with some degree of contempt by my tutor, who was constantly proclaiming that there was no truth in a concept unless it could be subjected to a repeatable experiment. He did not enlighten me as to the differing schools of thought, so I began to think that I was not suited to the study of psychology.

Winnicott had been invited by one of the student societies to give a paper. I had never heard of Winnicott, so it was by extreme good fortune that I attended his lecture. I had not realized how demoralized I had been made to feel by my tutor until I heard Winnicott's paper. For me, it was not just a "breath of fresh air", but more like the "kiss of life". Later, when discussing Winnicott's paper, my tutor's prejudice became very obvious to me, but worse still, I could see how much my tutor was concerned with my complying with his views rather than helping me to acquire knowledge and develop my own ideas. This, of course, was an old scare, for as a child I had been forced to develop a managing persona in the face of my parents' insistence on my complying. It was for that reason that I remember Winnicott saying, when he gave his next paper at Oxford, "I am allergic to propaganda". This comment was made in response to a student saying how Winnicott "ought" to think about some subject.

London School of Economics

I was very pleased, when I arrived at the London School of Economics and Political Science (L.S.E.) in 1964, to find that Winnicott was giving a series of seminars. It was during this period that I came to idealize him. He would always arrive early and sit looking at, and seemingly trying to evaluate, the group of students. After rubbing his face in a characteristic way he would *feel* his way into the subject. What he said was so much in tune with my feelings—in particular, my depression. It was also the case that Winnicott's positive view of the work of depression came to me with some degree of relief. His sense of fun was also very appealing. Winnicott was once asked: "With all your knowledge of children, wouldn't you sometimes like another chance at being a child?" Without any hesitation, he replied: "Once is quite enough."

My idealization of Winnicott reached its embarrassing zenith when, during an informal gathering, I said that as Winnicott was with us, rather than standing around talking about everyday things, we ought to be discussing more serious matters. Winnicott then quickly went on to tell us about an amusing event. During a consultation with a woman patient, she had asked to use the lavatory. Winnicott signalled that this would be all right, so the patient left the room. Winnicott then settled down on the couch, keeping half an ear open for the sound of the lavatory cistern. After a while, Winnicott's housekeeper came to the consulting-room door and hesitatingly knocked. She had been told never to do such a thing while Winnicott was working. The housekeeper apologized, but said that there was a woman at the front door, saying that she was in the middle of a session and therefore could she come in. Winnicott then learned that the patient had gone to the lavatory of the local railway station! It was only very much later that I realized that in response to my idealizing comments, Winnicott had, in effect, told a lavatory joke.

Towards the end of his series of seminars, however, I had an experience with Winnicott that considerably modified my attitude towards him. During the seminar, he had been describing the nature of the masculine and feminine parts of a little girl—in particular, her difficulty with her masculine identity. In the L.S.E. lift after the seminar I discussed with Winnicott how Jung had helpfully described the nature of the animus in girls. Winnicott seemed uncomfortable and said that Jung's idea was a good one, but that he tended not to use it. When I asked why, Winnicott said that he did not want to be thrown out of the Institute of Psycho-Analysis. At first I thought that he was joking. As someone once said of Winnicott, his anima was an actress. So I pushed him further on the matter. He said that he was not joking but would say no more. Could it be possible, I thought at the time, that a man of such ability and evident integrity could be cowed by an institution? This was too near my own struggle for me to just accept. While this exchange with Winnicott was not the only reason, there is no doubt that it played a very important part in my preference to train later on with the Society of Analytical Psychology.

Warlingham Park Hospital

Apart from attending many of his public talks, the next personal meeting that I had with Winnicott was just over a year later, when he gave a paper at Warlingham Park Hospital. The medical staff were not very sympathetic towards his approach, and one consultant was particularly hostile. The organizer of the meeting gave Winnicott a book token for the evening, and Winnicott later sent him a "thank you" letter, which the organizer showed to me. In my experience, his letters were carefully written, and in Winnicott's letter he said: "Thank you for the book token. After careful thought, I have decided to buy a copy of *Aggression in Animals*." The organizer did not miss the point!

In the evening of that talk at Warlingham Park Hospital, I gave Winnicott a lift to the railway station. Most of the time Winnicott seemed to travel by taxi. In the car, he talked about a woman reporter who had recently published an article about his work. During her interview she had asked him about his mother, and Winnicott had given one of his quick—perhaps too quick—answers: "Well, I had a mother, and that's all that can be said." The reporter printed his reply in her article, and it clearly upset Winnicott. In the car he kept asking me what I thought about the article and the reporter, adding that perhaps nobody would bother to read it. At that time, I had neither the experience nor the insight to make an appropriate comment, but I do remember wishing that I could ease his pain.

Individuation

The last time I met Winnicott was the evening that he gave the second of two papers on the subject of "individuation". The first paper was given by Frieda Fordham. When Winnicott arrived, rather than sitting "up front", he sat with the audience, in fact, near to where I was sitting. After nodding his hello, he said to me: "I came this evening because I thought that I would probably learn something." I was not very happy with Winnicott's paper because it seemed to be mostly a rehash of his already well-known ideas, put together in a hurry. I was somewhat reassured later when the chairman of that evening, Kenneth Lambert, showed me a letter from Winnicott apologizing for his paper. In the letter, which I hope still exists, Winnicott said that he thought that Frieda's paper had been very good and that the concept of "individuation" was a sound one. He also said that he was sorry about his paper not being very good, but that he had not given himself enough time to write it and he had "tried to get by 'by hook or by crook', and mostly by crook".

In recent years I have given more thought to what I saw at the time as Winnicott's impaired integrity in his relationship with the Institute of Psycho-Analysis. His reluctance to mention Jung or even to talk about some of Jung's concepts, which he clearly knew and, I think, used, activated my self-righteousness. We know how idealism can give rise to sadomasochistic excitement, and that we only maintain our idealism at other people's expense. As a young man, I was still projecting that part of my shadow in order to preserve my "high standards". With the passing of the years, I am now much more sympathetic towards the symptoms caused by survival anxieties in other people as well as my own. Fears in relation to survival cause many, if not all, institutions to locate the "good" as being inside and the "bad" as being outside. Pretending that the "bad out there" does not exist is one way of hoping that it will go away. Splitting, paranoia, and fighting are all born of fears in relation to survival, and at some time or another all institutions use these defences. Some of the time, individuals and institutions may feel strong enough to allow something in from the outside, but only if it is not too threatening to their identity. Of course, these threats are mostly exaggerated, but exaggeration, it seems to me, is only the negative side of creativity. In recent times, even Freud's integrity has been brought into question, and, as I have already implied, it is easy to be idealistic about others. In all this, we must return to Winnicott's idea of that which is "good enough". He said to me—and I believe to others—that he saw this as being his most important concept, and as I have grown, I have come to see more of its meaning—which was greatly enhanced when I came to see that this was Winnicott's way of describing the *coniunctio* between "good" and "bad". This is also another example of how Winnicott was able to translate complex analytic concepts into everyday language, which added considerably to their emotional impact.

I am sure that Winnicott was special for many people, and each person will have his or her own story to tell. It seems to me that he used his personal struggles and pain in a very creative way, and that resulted in his being able to speak to people in many ways and in many forms. For me, he was very facilitating, and for that I shall always be grateful.

CHAPTER TWELVE

D. W. Winnicott

David Holbrook

I met Donald Winnicott only once, on an occasion when he came to talk to an undergraduate society at the University of Cambridge. I was attending as a senior member. Before then, and afterward, I was in frequent correspondence with him, because he had become one of my major luminaries.

There were two reasons for this. One was that my wife was having psychotherapy and I was trying to adjust to this. I probably needed it more than she did, but, like most intellectuals, I wanted to study the problem theoretically, and someone—it may have been the professor of anthropology, Meyer Fortes, whose wife was a psychoanalyst—put me on to Winnicott. I was also working with the "bottom-stream" children at a secondary modern school (one of the Cambridgeshire Village Colleges), and these were presenting me with difficulties that were unbelievable until I began to understand some of their problems in the light of Winnicott's writings. I have written about these children in my book, *English for the Rejected: Training Literacy in the Lower Streams of the Secondary School* (Holbrook, 1964), which Winnicott read and liked.

Reading Winnicott helped me to overcome my doubts about psychotherapy in general and later enabled me to invoke ideas from psychoanalysis in literary criticism. I asked him for something that I could read, to put the whole movement into perspective, and he suggested the work of Harry Guntrip, which opened my eyes to the degree to which ideas behind psychotherapy had changed radically since the time of Freud. Surprisingly, Winnicott also suggested that I might profitably stay outside psychotherapy, as a personal experience, while I pursued my study of its theories. I was in communication frequently with Harry Guntrip, Masud Khan, and Peter Lomas, to whom I had been introduced by Winnicott. I found their comments and advice most helpful throughout the years.

At the time I met Winnicott, at that talk to the undergraduates, I was amazed by his energy and independence. He had driven down from London after a full day's work and insisted on driving home after the meeting—at about half past ten, I suppose. Off he went in his big Mercedes, into the darkness. Yet when we had climbed the steel staircase to the room where the meeting was held, he had paused frequently because of his heart condition. I remember some startlingly realistic remarks he made about his health before the meeting began.

I cannot now remember the title of his talk, or what it was about. But what I can remember is the experience of the impact of what he said. I already knew something of this effect from reading *Collected Papers: Through Paediatrics to Psycho-Analysis* (Winnicott, 1958a)—namely, the sense that something very original and illuminating was being said, which was beyond normal paradigms. It was this that gripped me whenever I read him.

As he spoke, you had the feeling that something outrageous had been said, something quite shocking, in a positive way, to which you now had to adjust. I suppose it must have been something like that famous remark: "There is no such thing as a baby." It was rather like being hit on the back of the head, though it was not painful or shocking—indeed, it had been said in the gentlest of tones and the most simple and direct language. But it came from a perspective that cut through the ordinary defences and obscurities and threw light on some aspect of experience to show it in a startling and vivid new light. There were several remarks of this kind. At first they seemed mad things for anyone to say, but then, as one came to terms with them, they changed one's view of life altogether, being the truths of inwardness. The nearest equivalent for me was the poetry of William Blake in, say, the *Songs of Innocence and Experience*: to point this out is to indicate the essence of Winnicott's work, its positive and creative concern with *being*.

Although Winnicott's writings and correspondence with me shed a great deal of illumination on the problems of my backward and disturbed pupils, they also made it clear to me that I had a personal problem. As a poet, novelist, and critic, I acclaimed love: but in my personal behaviour I was also guilty of falling into patterns of hate, beyond my own volition and without warning. And that hate came to be directed at the woman I loved, and this threatened to destroy my marriage, while the bottom would often fall out of my life: In fact, I encountered the problem of ambivalence. When our fourth and last child was born, I wrote to Winnicott tentatively confessing my anguish over this problem, and he wrote with characteristic if surprising directness the letter quoted "To a Confidant" (Winnicott, 1966a) in *The Spontaneous Gesture: Selected Letters of D. W. Winnicott* (Winnicott, 1987). The original letter reads as follows:

15th April, 1966

Dear Holbrook:

Thank you for your postcard. I think that you know the answer to your question because you have been in a state of primary maternal preoccupation relative to your new baby, and from what you write you have enjoyed the experience. Anthropologically you would recognise this under the term couvade, but it seems rather nasty to give a name to something that is being experienced in the present.

I wonder whether you can make use of this idea. Everybody is bisexual in the sense of the capacity to identify with man and woman. There is a great capacity for identification with a woman, and a similar but different thing, a male man with a split-off woman self. I have tried to refer to this in a paper which is not published but which you could look at if you liked, in which I talk about the male and female elements in men and women. Others of course have written on the same subject.

What strikes me is that in your own development you may be in the process of changing over from being a male with a split-off woman self to being a more integrated individual containing all the elements including the two identifications.

I think that the study of man's identification with woman has been very much complicated by a persistent attempt on the part of psycho-analysts to call everything that is not male in a man homosexuality, whereas in fact homosexuality is a secondary matter or less fundamental and rather a nuisance when one is trying to get at a man's woman identification.

I don't know whether you can make anything of this very condensed note but in any case there is always the waste paper basket.

Good wishes,

Yours sincerely,

D. W. Winnicott, F.R.C.P.

I do not remember what my original question had been, but Winnicott's response was one of the most illuminating I have ever received. His letter has that jokey tone, but it boldly lays its finger on a grave problem in one's emotional life—that is, on ambivalence, and on the problem of projection. I feel I have been writing about it ever since, both in fiction, and in criticism. I was only dimly aware of the dynamics by which one projects aspects of one's own make-up on to one's partner, and Winnicott's bold suggestion set my feet on a path that helped me, over the next twenty years, to overcome a destructive tendency that had threatened my family life. It seemed to me at the time a very chancy thing to say so suddenly to someone, but I suppose Winnicott took a studied risk and covered himself by that jokey tone. He sent me the paper to which he refers, and I have made much use of it both in my work and in my life (cf. Winnicott, 1972).

Perhaps he judged that—as he says somewhere—parents become strangely malleable when they have a new child. Certainly, my wife and I associate our growth towards harmony and peace with our last child, and what we learned from him. During his childhood, of course, we read *Therapeutic Consultations in Child Psychiatry* (Winnicott, 1971b), and *The Piggle: An Account of the*

Psycho-Analytic Treatment of a Little Girl (Winnicott, 1978). It is sad that Winnicott had no children of his own, since his insights contributed so enormously to the well-being of those whose parents read him and learned from him, about how much children suffer and also what brave and wonderful spirits they display—and how important it is to be able to enter into play with them, as he himself could, so marvellously.

CHAPTER THIRTEEN

Winnicottiana:
some hitherto unpublished documents

Brett Kahr

A sonnet by Barbara Dockar-Drysdale

I n 1958, Mrs Barbara Dockar-Drysdale, one of Winnicott's most devoted students and supervisees, wrote a poem: "A Sonnet for Winnicott". This poem moved Winnicott deeply; he did not throw it away but kept it preserved among his papers, and I found it in the Donald W. Winnicott Papers, in the Archives of Psychiatry at the Cornell Medical Center in New York City, New York. The initials "P.D.D." at the top of the poem stand for "Pip Dockar-Drysdale". All of Mrs Dockar-Drysdale's friends referred to her not as Barbara but, rather, as "Pip". Mrs Dockar-Drysdale seems to have written this during the Christmas period, and the poem concerns the abilities of young children. I have reproduced the poem without any alterations of punctuation or format. Mrs Dockar-Drysdale had not seen this poem in nearly 35 years. When I located it, I sent her a copy, and she told me how touched she felt to have had the opportunity to read the work again after all this time.

A sonnet for Winnicott
*from P.D.D.**

Within the compass of their skill they'll play
For you, yet must enclose each theme
With flute and pipe and drum, this Christmas day
They'll frame a carol, and—though it would seem
Their little hands could scarcely span a scale—
Yet in an octave they may yet succeed
In touching joy and sorrow, ease and pain,
That which is held and lost and found again.
While their small leader, slender stave in hand,
Knowing the narrow limits of their art,
Must ask no more than they can understand
Without a score. Yet if all play a part
They may yet blind a chord, still unaware
that notes have *clustered* in the frosty air.

Barbara [Pip] Dockar-Drysdale, 1958

A memorial speech by Clare Winnicott

In 1977, some six years after the death of Dr Donald Winnicott, his widow, Mrs Clare Winnicott, laid the foundation stone for the Donald Winnicott Centre, a specialist treatment unit for physically and mentally handicapped children at the Queen Elizabeth Hospital for Children in London's East End. During the 1920s and 1930s Winnicott used to work at the old Queen's Hospital for Children as an assistant physician, attached to both the general wards and to the London County Council Rheumatism Clinic. Clare Winnicott delivered the following address, previously unpublished. I have refrained from altering Mrs Winnicott's original spelling and punctuation. The assortment of errors contained in her typescript contributes to the charm of the document.

---

*This poem appears with the permission of Mrs Barbara Dockar-Drysdale and by the courtesy of the Archives of Psychiatry at The New York Hospital–Cornell Medical Center.

Donald Winnicott Centre
Queen Elizabeth Hospital for Children
Stone-laying Ceremony, Wednesday, 25th May 1977*

It is a great privilege to be invited to lay the foundation stone of the Donald Winnicott Centre, so named to commemorate his life and work and his connection with this Hospital. He had a great affection for "The Queen's" as it was then known, and many happy memories of his time here which he often talked of.

* * *

During the time that D.W. worked here—1923–33—he was also Physician in Charge of the L.C.C. Heart and Rheumatism Clinic for children, and held an appointment at the Paddington Green Children's Hospital. This latter post he held for forty years, and he reckoned that in total before he retired he had seen 60,000 mothers and children in one clinic or another. Apart from this he was also in practice as a Psycho-analyst of children and adults from the mid 1930's.

* * *

It has been suggested that I should briefly recall some of the special features of D.W.'s professional life and development.

* * *

He always said that one of the most profound influences in his life was the teaching of the well known Physician Sir Thomas Horder (later Lord Horder) when D.W. was a medical student at Bart's. It was Lord Horder who taught him the value of taking a careful detailed case history, and of *listening* to the patient, and not simply asking questions. This approach to his work (which implied an attitude) lasted him a lifetime, and was the main source of his continued learning and understanding. He approached each patient

---

*Speech reproduced by kind permission of the Contemporary Medical Archives Centre of The Wellcome Library for the History and Understanding of Medicine at The Wellcome Institute for the History of Medicine in London, and by courtesy of the Wellcome Trustees.

in order to find out about the patient and his illness, and not simply to impose his knowledge on to the situation.

* * *

The habit of listening to patients played a part in the development of D.W.'s *capacity to communicate* with parents and children which was one of his special gifts. A landmark in his career was the series of broadcast talks on aspects of Child Care and development which the B.B.C. invited him to give in the early 1940s. These were repeated, and were subsequently published. They brought him into touch with a wide section of the community, in this country and abroad, and he never refused to speak to any group which invited him.

* * *

In developing his way of communicating D.W. invented certain phrases, which embody concepts, of child care. Many of these have become familiar, and are part of the language of those involved personally or professionally in this field. I refer to such phrases as "The Ordinary Devoted Mother" "The Good Enough Mother" "The Facilitating Environment" "The Transitional Object"—this last referring to a child's first specially loved object which enables the child to reach out beyond the mother to the outside world. He felt this to be a vitally important area of experience, and the study of it was one of his main contributions to the general understanding of human growth and development.

* * *

It was while he was working at this hospital that D.W.'s interest in the *emotional aspects* of physical illness began to develop. This led to his gradual move "Through Paediatrics to Psycho-Analysis" (the title of his first book of collected papers), and it led him also into Child Pyschiatry [*sic*]. He was the first Paediatrician to make this kind of move, and it gave him the opportunity to contribute something first-hand from paediatrics to the theory and practice of psycho-analysis and child psychiatry. In this connection, his special use of the *therapeutic consultation* could be mentioned.

* * *

In the early days, D.W. needed time to study the emotional astects [sic] of illness in greater depth than could be done in a busy hospital clinic, and he told how he would invite hospital mothers and/or fathers, and pay their fares to visit him with their children in Harley Street. This unusual proceedure [sic] served two purposes—it made him feel more at home in Harley Street, where, as a young Consultant he had few patients, and was very ashamed of the fact—but the point is that it gave him the time that he needed with his patients to enable him to develop his own special interest and approach. He always felt how lucky he had been to be able to give that time so early in his career, and he was grateful to his father whose financial help enabled him to do so.

* * *

In 1931 D.W. published his first book *Clinical Notes on the Disorders of Childhood*. This was a first tentative attempt to take account of emotional factors in the study of childhood disorders. I am told that the book still has relevance, but at the time it seemed alarming to the reviewers who reached the conclusion: "this man is dangerous". In other words, this was a new way of looking at childhood disorders, and was therefore under suspicion. But he survived this set-back, and went on to write many more books and papers based on his clinical findings. He was essentially a clinician, and remained in practice to the end of his life.

* * *

I would like to think that the Donald Winnicott Centre will go on with the kind of work that he enjoyed and believed in, and will combine the psycho-analytic approach and insight into stress situations and developmental problems, together with the skilled specialist knowledge needed to provide a comprehensive assessment and treatment centre for children in this area of London. Nothing could more appropiately [sic] commemorate the work of someone who tried to look at patients not in terms of one speciality or another, but in terms of their total need as individuals within a given family and social setting. The importance of the family structure to the development of the individual child was something that D.W. learnt from psycho-analysis and brought with him into his paediatric practice.

* * *

I hope that all who work at the Donald Winnicott Centre will enjoy their work as much as he did, and that all who come here, parents and children, will find the professional help and care that they need.

Clare Winnicott
May, 1977

Selected Correspondence
with Dr Charles Rycroft

The late Dr Charles Rycroft, the distinguished psychotherapist and author, proved very genial and gracious to me throughout the many years of my research on the life of Dr Donald Winnicott. Dr Rycroft knew Winnicott well during the course of his work at the British Psycho-Analytical Society and the Institute of Psycho-Analysis, and he shared many memories with me from the period of his association with Winnicott. Several years before his death on 24 May 1998, Dr Rycroft generously permitted me to inspect his letters from Winnicott, and he had authorized me to reprint some of these hitherto unpublished letters, which shed light on Winnicott's scientific interests during the 1950s. Once again, I have reproduced Winnicott's letters in their exact form, retaining any errors of spelling or punctuation for the sake of authenticity.

Letter 1 (typed)

5th February 1954

Dr C.F. Rycroft,
6 Park Crescent,
W.1.

My dear Rycroft,
This is a general letter about Training matters and I think that the best thing would be for it to be followed up by our spending an evening together if you are not too busy. I would very much like it if you could come here for an hour or two one evening.

The fact is that although I am apparently well on the road to recovery and doing half-time work, I would very much like to be relieved of Training Committee matters. You have agreed in principle to take over this work and I think we shall have no difficulty whatever in sharing some of the work until the summer. If you can do it all, I would like to pass on the whole thing to you, but in that case I would of course be willing to help you out whenever you need it.

There is really not an awful lot that is absolutely necessary in regard to Training Secretary work although a great deal could be done; certainly I have not done it. The main trouble has been the interviewing of all the people who write for information. I have enjoyed this very much as it has given me a range of experience which I would not otherwise have had. On the other hand, one must live in order to be able to benefit from experience. I think that the majority of applications for this year have now been already made and any enquiries coming in at the present time are on the whole of the sporadic and not very interesting variety. Unless you protest, I shall hand on to you all the letters which ordinarily I would follow up by interview.

The next question is would it be best for you to act as Secretary altogether, with me turning up when possible on the Training Committee? I know that I would welcome this if you can do it without too much strain as I am not really fit to do much evening work, certainly not staying late. On the other hand, there are certain training problems that I am very interested in and I want to retain my place on the Training Committee.

A comment that I would like to make is that as Training Secretary I found it rather a relief to discover that one is really in some ways not so much in a responsible position, because in order to be fair to all the various political parties one simply has to act almost mechanically according to the rules as the servant of the Committee. There are many occasions when I would express my personal view very much more strongly if I had not been Secretary. The great point in the Secretary work is to do nothing which can make the various groupings start playing for position, so that one has the freedom to allot students in the ordinary sensible way as vacancies occur. I am sure you know what tremendous tensions arise if there comes any sort of moment at which one has roused the political issue by indiscretion.

If you have time for this, I think you may find it quite interesting and I am writing to see how much sanction I can get from you for handing over the work to you subject to the approval of the Training Committee.

Yours very sincerely,

[signed].

D. W. Winnicott

Letter 2 (hand-written)

7 Oct 1956

Dear Rycroft, (qua Sci Sec)

If you find empty spaces:

(1) A psycho-somatic evening is long overdue. We need a statement of our position.

(2) "The psycho analyst as consultant psychiatrist" would give another important discussion, which ties up with

(3) Child psychiatry and psychoanalysis.

Also

(4) I would like to throw a word at the society like "black" (as in the Medical Section when I was president) to see what the Society makes of it — + to bring in back-benchers. Or, perhaps, "ghost" would be better.

I might have other ideas

Yours

D. W. Winnicott

[Winnicott wrote the following notes on the left- and right-hand margins of the stationery]:

Not expecting reply—

Actually I liked the Bion [illegible] but its difficult to get the proper discussion sorry I fear.

Letter 3 (typed)

17th October 1956

Dr C.F. Rycroft,
2 Park Crescent,
W.1.

Dear Rycroft,

I handed you a note the other evening about adolescents. It seems to me not only a good idea that we should discuss adolescents but also I feel that this might be a way of bringing in Miss Freud. Perhaps she would lead off a symposium or give a full-length paper on the main theme of psycho-analysis and psycho-analytic theory. I should think that there would be a large number of people who would like to help develop this theme. It might be possible to get someone to scour the literature which I think is not very great.

There are a few odd people who have had experience with adolescents, such as Oscar Friedmann; also Miss Hellmann has had a series of adolescent boys in analysis.

All for now,

Yours,

[signed].

Letter 4 (typed)

17th January 1957

Dr Charles Rycroft,
2 Park Crescent, W.1.

Dear Dr. Rycroft,

I would like you to know that I did enjoy your paper last night. It had several merits, being clear and not too long, and I think the discussion was interesting although sticky at one patch. I am sure you will go on thinking out how to make more use of the theme.

As I said at the time, I am most interested in the part which deals with the build-up of the idea of a whole person each way round, as I think that analysis throws light on this aspect of early "signs" in the study of this subject although to some extent the process takes place through the content of the interpretations.

Looking back, I am sorry I made people laugh, and I hope that this was not one of the causes for the stickiness in the beginning of the discussion. I am taking a long time to learn how to preside.
Good wishes,
Yours,
[signed]
D. W. Winnicott

[*Editorial note*: Dr Charles Rycroft kindly identified the paper to which Winnicott has referred in this letter of 17 January 1957 as Rycroft's essay on "An Enquiry into the Function of Words in the Psycho-Analytical Situation", which he had presented to the British Psycho-Analytical Society on 16 January 1957. Rycroft's (1958) contribution appeared one year later in the *International Journal of Psycho-Analysis*.]

REFERENCES

Abram, J. (1996). *The Language of Winnicott: A Dictionary of Winnicott's Use of Words.* London: Karnac.

Alvarez, A. (1992). *Live Company: Psychoanalytic Psychotherapy with Autistic, Borderline, Deprived and Abused Children.* London: Routledge.

Anand, K. J. S., & Hickey, P. R. (1987). Pain and its effects in the human neonate and fetus. *New England Journal of Medicine, 317*: 1322.

Anthony, E. J., & Benedek, T. (Eds.) (1970). *Parenthood: Its Psychology and Psychopathology.* Boston, MA: Little, Brown and Company.

Anthony, E. J., & Pollock, G. H. (Eds.) (1985). *Parental Influences in Sickness and in Health.* Boston, MA: Little, Brown and Company.

Astington, J. W., & Gopnik, A. (1991). Theoretical explanations of children's understanding of the mind. *British Journal of Developmental Psychology, 9*: 7–31.

Balint, M. (1968). *The Basic Fault: Therapeutic Aspects of Regression.* London: Tavistock Publications.

Barcroft, J. (1947). *Researches in Pre-Natal Life. Volume 1.* Springfield, IL: Charles C Thomas.

Barrett, J. H. W. (1982). Prenatal influences on adaptation in the newborn. In: P. Stratton (Ed.), *Psychobiology of the Human Newborn* (pp. 267–295). Chichester, Sussex: John Wiley and Sons.

Bartels, H. (1970). *Prenatal Respiration.* New York: John Wiley and Sons.

Bick, E. (1964). Notes on infant observation in psycho-analytic training. *International Journal of Psycho-Analysis, 45:* 558–566.

Bick, E. (1968). The experience of the skin in early object relations. *International Journal of Psycho-Analysis, 49:* 484–486.

Blum, T. (1993). Early proto-developmental enrichment stimulations and possible changes in the functional morphology of the brain. In: T. Blum & D. Yew (Eds.), *Human Prenatal Brain Development.* Berlin: Leonardo Publishers.

Bollas, C. (1987). *The Shadow of the Object: Psychoanalysis of the Unthought Known.* London: Free Association Books.

Bonomi, C. (1994). Why have we ignored Freud the "paediatrician"? The relevance of paediatric training for the origins of psychoanalysis. In: A. Haynal & E. Falzeder (Eds.), *100 Years of Psychoanalysis: Contributions to the History of Psychoanalysis* (pp. 55–99). Geneva: Institutions Universitaires de Psychiatrie de Genève.

Boylan, P., & Lewis, P. J. (1980). Fetal breathing in labor. *Obstetrics and Gynecology, 56:* 35–38.

Bradley, R. M., & Mistretta, C. M. (1975). Fetal sensory receptors. *Physiological Reviews, 55:* 358.

Brafman, A. H. (1988). Infant observation. *International Review of Psycho-Analysis, 15:* 45–59.

Brazelton, T. B., & Cramer, B. G. (1990). *The Earliest Relationship.* New York: Addison-Wesley Publication Company.

Briend, A. (1979). Fetal malnutrition: the price of upright posture? *British Medical Journal, 2:* 317–319.

Brodsky, J. (1987). *Less Than One.* London: Penguin Books.

Carter-Jessop, L., & Keller, B. (1987). Early maternal bonding. In: T. R. Verny (Ed.), *Pre- and Perinatal Psychology: An Introduction* (pp. 107–127). New York: Human Sciences Press.

Casement, P. J. (1985). *On Learning from the Patient.* London: Tavistock Publications.

Chamberlain, D. B. (1988). *Babies Remember Birth.* Los Angeles, CA: Jeremy P. Tarcher.

Chamberlain, D. B. (1992). Babies are not what we thought: call for a new paradigm. *International Journal of Prenatal and Perinatal Studies, 4:* 168–169.

Chamberlain, D. B. (1993a). Prenatal intelligence. In: T. Blum (Ed.), *Prenatal Perception, Learning and Bonding* (pp. 14–21). Berlin: Leonardo Publishers.

Chamberlain, D. B. (1993b). How pre- and perinatal psychology can transform the world. *International Journal of Prenatal and Perinatal Psychology and Medicine, 5:* 413–424.

Child at Risk: A Report of the Standing Senate Committee on Health, Welfare and Science (1980). Quebec: Canadian Government Publishing Center.

Damasio, A. R. (1994). *Descartes' Error: Emotion, Reason, and the Human Brain.* New York: G. P. Putnam's Sons.

Davies, J. M., & Frawley, M. G. (1994). *Treating Adult Survivors of Childhood Sexual Abuse.* New York: Basic Books.

DeCasper, A. J. (1984). Studying learning in the womb. *Science, 225:* 384.

DeCasper, A. J., & Fifer, W. P. (1980). Of human bonding: newborns prefer their mothers' voices. *Science, 208:* 1174–1176.

deMause, L. (1981). The fetal origins of history. *Journal of Psychohistory, 9,* 1–89.

Dockar-Drysdale, B. (1974). My debt to Winnicott. In: B. Dockar-Drysdale, *The Provision of Primary Experience: Winnicottian Work with Children and Adolescents* (pp. 1–6). London: Free Association Books, 1990.

Efron, A. (1985). The sexual body: an interdisciplinary perspective. *Journal of Mind and Behavior, 6:* 118–121.

Erikson, E. H. (1950). *Childhood and Society.* New York: W.W. Norton and Company.

Ferreira, A. J. (1960). The pregnant woman's emotional attitude and its reflection on the newborn. *American Journal of Orthopsychiatry, 30:* 553–556.

Fifer, W. P. (1987). Neonatal preference for mother's voice. In: N. A. Krasnegor et al. (Eds.), *Perinatal Development: A Psychobiological Perspective* (pp. 111–115). New York: Academic Press.

Fodor, N. (1949). *The Search for the Beloved: A Clinical Investigation of the Trauma of Birth and Prenatal Condition.* New Hyde Park, NY: University Books.

Fraiberg, S. (1982). Pathological defenses in infancy. *Psychoanalytic Quarterly, 51:* 612–634.

Freeman, M. (1987). Is infant learning egocentric or duocentric? Was Piaget wrong? *Pre- and Peri-Natal Psychology Journal, 2:* 25–42.

Freud, A. (1965). *Normality and Pathology in Childhood: Assessments of Development.* London: Hogarth Press and the Institute of Psycho-Analysis.

Freud, S. (1895d), with J. Breuer. *Studies on Hysteria.* In: *The Standard Edition of the Complete Psychological Works of Sigmund Freud. Volume*

II (1893–1895). *Studies on Hysteria* (ed. and transl. J. Strachey, A. Freud, A. Strachey, & A. Tyson). London: Hogarth Press and the Institute of Psycho-Analysis, 1955.

Freud, S. (1900a). *The Interpretation of Dreams*. In: *Standard Edition, Volumes IV & V*. London: Hogarth Press and the Institute of Psycho-Analysis, 1953.

Freud, S. (1920g). *Beyond the Pleasure Principle*. In: *Standard Edition, Volume XVIII*. London: Hogarth Press and the Institute of Psycho-Analysis, 1953.

Freud, S. (1926). *Inhibitions, Symptoms and Anxiety*. In: *Standard Edition, Volume XX*. London: Hogarth Press and the Institute of Psycho-Analysis, 1953.

Goldman, D. (1993). *In Search of the Real: The Origins and Originality of D. W. Winnicott*. Northvale, NJ: Jason Aronson.

Goodlin, R. C. (1979). *Care of the Fetus*. New York: Masson Publishing.

Gorer, G., & Rickman, J. (1949). *The People of Great Russia: A Psychological Study*. London: Cresset Press.

Grof, S. (1985). *Beyond the Brain: Birth, Death, and Transcendence in Psychotherapy*. Albany, NY: State University of New York.

Hamilton, V. (1981). *Narcissus and Oedipus: The Children of Psychoanalysis*. London: Routledge and Kegan Paul.

Herrenkohl, L. R. (1982). The anxiety-prone personality: effects of prenatal stress on the infant. In: R. J. Mathew (Ed.), *The Biology of Anxiety* (pp. 51–86). New York: Brunner/Mazel.

Holbrook, D. (1964). *English for the Rejected: Training Literacy in the Lower Streams of the Secondary School*. London: Cambridge University Press.

Hopkins, J. (1986). Solving the mystery of monsters: steps towards the recovery from trauma. *Journal of Child Psychotherapy, 13*: 61–72.

Humphrey, T. (1970). Function of the nervous system during prenatal life. In: U. Stave (Ed.), *Physiology of the Perinatal Period. Volume 2* (pp. 754–789). New York: Appleton-Century-Crofts.

Ianniruberto, A., & Tajani, E. (1981). Ultrasonographic study of fetal movements. *Seminars in Perinatology, 5*: 175–181.

Jacobson, B. (1988). Perinatal origin of eventual self-destructive behavior. *Pre- and Peri-Natal Psychology, 2*: 227–241.

Janov, A. (1973). *The Feeling Child*. New York: Simon and Schuster.

Jones, E. (1916). The theory of symbolism. *British Journal of Psychology, 9*: 181–229.

Jones, E. (1927). The early development of female sexuality. *International Journal of Psycho-Analysis, 8*: 459–472.

Kahr, B. (1996a). *D. W. Winnicott: A Biographical Portrait.* London: Karnac.

Kahr, B. (1996b). Donald Winnicott and the foundations of child psychotherapy. *Journal of Child Psychotherapy, 22:* 327–342.

Kahr, B. (in press). Juvenile paedophilia: the psychodynamics of young sex offenders. In: C. Socarides, S. Kramer, K. Gould & A. Freedman (Eds.), *The Sexual Deviations: Psychoanalytic Theory and Therapy.* Madison, CT: International Universities Press.

Khan, M. M. R. (1988). *When Spring Comes: Awakenings in Clinical Psychoanalysis.* London: Chatto and Windus.

Klein, M. (1932). *Die Psychoanalyse des Kindes.* Vienna: Internationaler Psychoanalytischer Verlag.

Klein, M. (1952). On observing the behaviour of young infants. In: M. Klein, P. Heimann, S. Isaacs, & J. Riviere (Eds.), *Developments in Psycho-Analysis* (pp. 237–270). London: Hogarth Press.

LaGoy, L. (1993). The loss of a twin in utero's effect on pre-natal and post-natal bonding. *International Journal of Prenatal and Perinatal Psychology and Medicine, 5:* 439–444.

Laing, R. D. (1960). *The Divided Self: A Study of Sanity and Madness.* London: Tavistock Publications.

Langs, R. (1992a). *A Clinical Workbook for Psychotherapists.* London: Karnac.

Langs, R. (1992b). *Science, Systems and Psychoanalysis.* London: Karnac.

Langs, R. (1993a). *Empowered Psychotherapy.* London: Karnac.

Langs, R. (1993b). Psychoanalysis: narrative myth or narrative science? *Contemporary Psychoanalysis, 29:* 555–594.

Langs, R. (1995). *Clinical Practice and the Architecture of the Mind.* London: Karnac.

LeDoux, J. E. (1994). Emotion, memory and the brain. *Scientific American* (June): 50–57.

Lewis, P. J., & Boylan, P. (1979). Fetal breathing: a review. *American Journal of Obstetrics and Gynecology, 134:* 270–275.

Lieberman, N. (1983). Early development of stress and later behavior. *Science, 1141,* 824.

Liley, A. W. (1972). The foetus as personality. *Australian and New Zealand Journal of Psychiatry, 6:* 99–105.

Mahler, M. S., Pine, F., & Bergman, A. (1975). *The Psychological Birth of the Human Infant: Symbiosis and Individuation.* New York: Basic Books.

Maiwald, M., & Janus, L. (1993) . Development, behavior and psychic experience in the prenatal period and the consequences for life history: a bibliographic survey. *International Journal of Prenatal and Perinatal Psychology and Medicine, 5:* 451–485.

McDougall, J. (1989). *Theatres of the Body: A Psychoanalytic Approach to Psychosomatic Illness*. London: Free Association Books.

Mednick, S. A. (1971). Birth defects and schizophrenia. *Psychology Today*, 4: 48–50.

Middlebrook, D. W. (1991). *Anne Sexton: A Biography*. Boston, MA: Houghton Mifflin Company.

Miller, L., Rustin, M., Rustin, M., & Shuttleworth, J. (Eds.) (1989). *Closely Observed Infants*. London: Gerald Duckworth and Company.

Milner, M. (1972). For Dr. Winnicott Memorial Meeting 19 January 1972. *The British Psycho-Analytical Society and The Institute of Psycho-Analysis. Scientific Bulletin*, 57: 5–10.

Milner, M. (1978). D.W. Winnicott and the two-way journey. In: S. A. Grolnick, L. Barkin, & W. Muensterberger (Eds.), *Between Reality and Fantasy: Transitional Objects and Phenomena* (pp. 37–42). New York: Jason Aronson.

Norwood, C. (1980). *At Highest Risk: Environmental Hazards to Young and Unborn Children*. New York: McGraw-Hill.

Orbach, S. (1986). *Hunger Strike: The Anorectic's Struggle as a Metaphor for Our Age*. London: Faber and Faber.

Orbach, S. (1994). Working with the false body. In: A. Erskine & D. Judd (Eds.), *The Imaginative Body: Psychodynamic Therapy in Health Care* (pp. 165–179). London: Whurr Publishers.

Orbach, S. (1995). Countertransference and the false body. In: *Winnicott Studies, Vol. 10* (pp. 3–13). London: Karnac.

Osterweil, E. (1990). "A Psychoanalytic Exploration of Fetal Mental Development and its Role in the Origin of Object Relations." Doctoral Dissertation, California Graduate Institute.

Osterweil, E. (1993). "Notes on the Vicissitudes of Intrauterine Experience." Unpublished typescript.

Parker, R. (1994). Maternal ambivalence. *Winnicott Studies*, 9, 3–17.

Parker, R. (1995). *Torn in Two: The Experience of Maternal Ambivalence*. London: Virago Press.

Phillips, A. (1988). *Winnicott*. London: Fontana.

Pines, D. (1980). Skin communication: early skin disorders and their effect on transference and countertransference. *International Journal of Psycho-Analysis*, 61: 315–323.

Piontelli, A. (1988). Pre-natal life and birth as reflected in the analysis of a 2-year-old psychotic girl. *International Review of Psycho-Analysis*, 15: 73–81.

Piontelli, A. (1992). *From Fetus to Child: An Observational and Psychoanalytical Study*. London: Tavistock/Routledge.

Racker, H. (1968). *Transference and Countertransference*. London: Hogarth Press and the Institute of Psycho-Analysis.

Rank, O. (1924). *Das Trauma der Geburt und seine Bedeutung für die Psychoanalyse*. Vienna: Internationaler Psychoanalytischer Verlag.

Rascovsky, A. (1977). *El psiquismo Fetal*. Buenos Aires: Editorial Paidos.

Roazen, P. (1990). Tola Rank. *Journal of the American Academy of Psychoanalysis, 18*: 247–259.

Roedding, J. (1991). Birth trauma and suicide: a study of the relationship between near-death experiences at birth and later suicidal behavior. *Pre- and Peri-Natal Psychology Journal, 6*: 145–169.

Rosenfeld, E. (1970). Letter to Donald W. Winnicott. 28 November. Box 8. File 13. Donald W. Winnicott Papers. Archives of Psychiatry. History of Psychiatry Section. Department of Psychiatry. The Oskar Diethelm Library of the History of Psychiatry. The New York Hospital. Cornell Medical Center. New York, NY.

Rycroft, C. (1958). An enquiry into the function of words in the psychoanalytical situation. *International Journal of Psycho-Analysis, 39*: 408–415.

Ryle, A. (1990). *Cognitive Analytic Therapy: Active Participation in Change*. Chichester, Sussex: John Wiley and Sons.

Sandler, J. (1976). Countertransference and role-responsiveness. *International Review of Psycho-Analysis, 3*: 43–47.

Scarf, M. (1976). *Body, Mind, Behavior*, New York: Dell Publishing.

Schier, K. (1993). The analysis of appearance and meaning of prenatal and perinatal phantasies in the psychoanalytically oriented psychotherapy of children. *International Journal of Prenatal and Perinatal Psychology and Medicine, 5*: 433–438.

Share, L. (1994). *If Someone Speaks, It Gets Lighter: Dreams and the Reconstruction of Infant Trauma*. Hillsdale, NJ: Analytic Press.

Sinason, V. (1992). *Mental Handicap and the Human Condition: New Approaches from the Tavistock*. London: Free Association Books.

Sontag, L. (1965). Implications of fetal behavior and environment for adult personalities. *Annals of the New York Academy of Sciences, 134*: 782–786.

Spelt, D. (1948). The conditioning of the human fetus in utero. *Journal of Experimental Psychology, 38*: 338–346.

Stainton, M. C. (1985). The fetus: a growing member of the family. *Family Relations, 34*: 321–326.

Stevenson, R. E. (1977). *The Fetus and Newly Born Infant: Influences of the Prenatal Environment*. Second Edition. St. Louis, MO: C. V. Mosby.

Stott, O. H. (1977). Follow-up study from birth of effects of prenatal stress. *Developmental Medicine and Child Neurology, 15*: 770–787.

Strachey, A. (1924). Letter to James Strachey. 29 December. In: P. Meisel & W. Kendrick (Eds.), *Bloomsbury/Freud: The Letters of James and Alix Strachey, 1924–1925* (pp. 262–263). New York: Basic Books. 1985.

Subbotsky, E. V. (1993). *Foundations of the Mind: Children's Understanding of Reality.* Cambridge, MA: Harvard University Press.

Trowell, J., & Miles, G. (1991). The contribution of observation training to professional development in social work. *Social Work Practice, 5:* 51–60.

Trowell, J., & Rustin, M. (1991). Developing the internal observer in professionals in training. *Infant Mental Health Journal, 23:* 233–235.

van de Carr, R., & Lehrer, M. (1992). *The Prenatal Classroom: A Parent's Guide for Teaching Their Preborn Baby.* Atlanta, GA: Humanics Publishing Group.

van der Kolk, B. A. (1988). The trauma spectrum: the interaction of biological and social events in the genesis of the trauma response. *Journal of Traumatic Stress, 1:* 273–290.

Varma, V. (Ed.) (1974). *Psychotherapy Today.* London: Constable and Company.

Varma, V. (Ed.) (1993). *How and Why Children Hate.* London: Jessica Kingsley Publishers.

Verny, T. R. (Ed.) (1987). *Pre- and Perinatal Psychology: An Introduction.* New York: Human Sciences Press.

Verny, T. R. (1989). The scientific basis of pre- and peri-natal psychology: Part 1. *Pre- and Peri-Natal Psychology Journal, 3:* 162–164.

Vizard, E., Monck, E., & Misch, P. (1995). Child and adolescent sex abuse perpetrators: a review of the research literature. *Journal of Child Psychology and Psychiatry and Allied Disciplines, 36:* 731–756.

Vizard, E., Wynick, S., Hawkes, C., Woods, J., & Jenkins, J. (1996). Juvenile sexual offenders: assessment issues. *British Journal of Psychiatry, 168:* 259–262.

Ward, A. J. (1991). Prenatal stress and childhood psychopathology. *Child Psychiatry and Human Development, 22:* 97–110.

Winnicott, D. W. (1931). *Clinical Notes on Disorders of Childhood.* London: William Heinemann (Medical Books).

Winnicott, D. W. (1941). The observation of infants in a set situation. *International Journal of Psycho-Analysis, 22:* 229–249.

Winnicott, D. W. (1943a). Delinquency research. *The New Era in Home and School, 24:* 65–67.

Winnicott, D. W. (1943b). Treatment of mental disease by induction of fits. In: D. W. Winnicott (1989). *Psycho-Analytic Explorations* (ed. C. Winnicott, R. Shepherd, & M. Davis) (pp. 516–521). London: Karnac.

Winnicott, D. W. (1944a). What about father? In: D. W. Winnicott, *Getting to Know Your Baby* (pp. 16–21). London: William Heinemann (Medical Books), 1945.

Winnicott, D. W. (1944b). Introduction to a symposium on the psychoanalytic contribution to the theory of shock therapy. In: D. W. Winnicott (1989). *Psycho-Analytic Explorations* (ed. C. Winnicott, R. Shepherd, & M. Davis) (pp. 525–528). London: Karnac.

Winnicott, D. W. (1944c). Kinds of psychological effect of shock therapy. In: D. W. Winnicott (1989). *Psycho-Analytic Explorations* (ed. C. Winnicott, R. Shepherd, & M. Davis) (pp. 529–533). London: Karnac.

Winnicott, D. W. (1945a). *Getting to Know Your Baby*. London: William Heinemann (Medical Books).

Winnicott, D. W. (1945b). Primitive emotional development. *International Journal of Psycho-Analysis, 26*: 137–143.

Winnicott, D. W. (1945c). The evacuated child. In: D. W. Winnicott (1957). *The Child and the Outside World: Studies in Developing Relationships* (ed. Janet Hardenberg) (pp. 83–87). London: Tavistock Publications.

Winnicott, D. W. (1948). Children's hostels in war and peace: a contribution to the symposium on "Lessons for Child Psychiatry". Given at a Meeting of the Medical Section of the British Psychological Society, 27 February 1946. *British Journal of Medical Psychology, 21*: 175–180.

Winnicott, D. W. (1949a) Hate in the counter-transference. *International Journal of Psycho-Analysis: 30*: 69–74.

Winnicott, D. W. (1949b). Birth memories, birth trauma, and anxiety. In: D. W. Winnicott, *Collected Papers: Through Paediatrics to Psycho-Analysis* (pp. 174–193). London: Tavistock Publications, 1958.

Winnicott, D. W. (1949c). Letter to Paul Federn. 3 January. In: D. W. Winnicott, *The Spontaneous Gesture: Selected Letters of D. W. Winnicott* (ed. F. R. Rodman) (p. 12). Cambridge, MA: Harvard University Press, 1987.

Winnicott, D. W. (1953). Transitional objects and transitional phenomena: a study of the first not-me possession. *International Journal of Psycho-Analysis, 34*: 89–97.

Winnicott, D. W. (1954). Mind and its relation to the psyche–soma. *British Journal of Medical Psychology, 27*: 201–209.

Winnicott, D. W. (1955). Metapsychological and clinical aspects of regression within the psycho-analytical set-up. *International Journal of Psycho-Analysis, 36*: 16–26.

Winnicott, D. W. (1956). The antisocial tendency. In: D. W. Winnicott,

Collected Papers: Through Paediatrics to Psycho-Analysis (pp. 306–315). London: Tavistock Publications, 1958.

Winnicott, D. W. (1957). On the contribution of direct child observation to psycho-analysis. In: D. W. Winnicott (1965a). *The Maturational Processes and the Facilitating Environment: Studies in the Theory of Emotional Development* (pp. 109–114). London: Hogarth Press and the Institute of Psycho-Analysis.

Winnicott, D. W. (1958a). *Collected Papers: Through Paediatrics to Psycho-Analysis.* London: Tavistock Publications.

Winnicott, D. W. (1958b). The capacity to be alone. *International Journal of Psycho-Analysis, 39*: 298-304.

Winnicott, D. W. (1960a). String. *Journal of Child Psychology and Psychiatry and Allied Disciplines, 1*: 49–52.

Winnicott, D. W. (1960b). The theory of the parent–infant relationship. *International Journal of Psycho-Analysis, 41*: 585–595.

Winnicott, D. W. (1960c). Ego distortion in terms of True and False Self. In: D. W. Winnicott, *The Maturational Processes and the Facilitating Environment: Studies in the Theory of Emotional Development* (pp. 140–152). London: Hogarth Press and the Institute of Psycho-Analysis, 1965.

Winnicott, D. W. (1961). Varieties of psychotherapy. In: D. W. Winnicott, *Deprivation and Delinquency* (ed. C. Winnicott, R. Shepherd, & M. Davis) (pp. 232–240). London: Tavistock Publications, 1984.

Winnicott, D. W. (1963a). Dependence in infant care, in child care, and in the psycho-analytic setting. *International Journal of Psycho-Analysis, 44*: 339-344.

Winnicott, D. W. (1963b). From dependence towards independence in the development of the individual. In: D. W. Winnicott, *The Maturational Processes and the Facilitating Environment: Studies in the Theory of Emotional Development* (pp. 83–92). London: Hogarth Press and the Institute of Psycho-Analysis, 1965.

Winnicott, D. W. (1963c). Psychiatric disorder in terms of infantile maturational processes. In: D. W. Winnicott, *The Maturational Processes and the Facilitating Environment: Studies in the Theory of Emotional Development* (pp. 230–241). London: Hogarth Press and the Institute of Psycho-Analysis, 1965.

Winnicott, D. W. (1964a). The value of depression. *British Journal of Psychiatric Social Work, 7*: 123–127.

Winnicott, D. W. (1964b). Book Review of Carl Gustav Jung. *Memories, Dreams, Reflections. International Journal of Psycho-Analysis, 45*: 450–455.

Winnicott, D. W. (1965). *The Maturational Processes and the Facilitating*

Environment: Studies in the Theory of Emotional Development. London: Hogarth Press and the Institute of Psycho-Analysis.

Winnicott, D. W. (1966a). Letter to M. 15 April. In: D. W. Winnicott, *The Spontaneous Gesture: Selected Letters of D. W. Winnicott* (ed. F. R. Rodman) (p. 155). Cambridge, MA: Harvard University Press, 1987.

Winnicott, D. W. (1966b). Letter to K. R. Llewellin. 20 October. Box 6. File 5. Donald W. Winnicott Papers. Archives of Psychiatry. History of Psychiatry Section. Department of Psychiatry. The Oskar Diethelm Library of the History of Psychiatry. The New York Hospital. Cornell Medical Center. New York, NY.

Winnicott, D. W. (1966c). Letter to Michael Balint. 8 December. Box 6. File 1. Donald W. Winnicott Papers. Archives of Psychiatry. History of Psychiatry Section. Department of Psychiatry. The Oskar Diethelm Library of the History of Psychiatry. The New York Hospital. Cornell Medical Center. New York, NY.

Winnicott, D. W. (1967). Preliminary Notes for "Communication between infant and mother, mother and infant, compared and contrasted". In: D. W. Winnicott, *Babies and Their Mothers* (ed. C. Winnicott, R. Shepherd, & M. Davis) (pp. 107–109). Reading, MA: Addison-Wesley Publishing Company, 1987.

Winnicott, D. W. (1968a). Playing: its theoretical status in the clinical situation. *International Journal of Psycho-Analysis, 49*: 591–599.

Winnicott, D. W. (1968b). Delinquency as a sign of hope. *Prison Service Journal: 7*, 2–9.

Winnicott, D. W. (1968c). Letter to David Holbrook. 25 January. Box 7. File 3. Donald W. Winnicott Papers. Archives of Psychiatry. History of Psychiatry Section. Department of Psychiatry. The Oskar Diethelm Library of the History of Psychiatry. The New York Hospital. Cornell Medical Center. New York, NY.

Winnicott, D. W. (1969a). The use of an object. *International Journal of Psycho-Analysis, 50*: 711–716.

Winnicott, D. W. (1969b). Freedom. In: D. W. Winnicott, *Home is Where We Start From: Essays by a Psychoanalyst* (ed. C. Winnicott, R. Shepherd, & M. Davis) (pp. 228–238). Harmondsworth, Middlesex: Penguin Books, 1986.

Winnicott, D. W. (1970). The mother–infant experience of mutuality. In: E. J. Anthony & T. Benedek (Eds.), *Parenthood: Its Psychology and Psychopathology* (pp. 245–256). Boston, MA: Little, Brown.

Winnicott, D. W. (1971a). *Playing and Reality.* London: Tavistock Publications.

Winnicott, D. W. (1971b). *Therapeutic Consultations in Child Psychiatry.* London: Hogarth Press and the Institute of Psycho-Analysis.

Winnicott, D. W. (1971c). The concept of a healthy personality. In: J. D. Sutherland (Ed.), *Towards Community Mental Health* (pp. 1–15). London: Tavistock Publications.

Winnicott, D. W. (1972). Split-off male and female elements found clinically in men and women: theoretical inferences. *Psychoanalytic Forum, 4:* 362–379. New York: International Universities Press.

Winnicott, D. W. (1974). Fear of breakdown. *International Review of Psycho-Analysis, 1:* 103–107.

Winnicott, D. W. (1978). *The Piggle: An Account of the Psycho-Analytic Treatment of a Little Girl.* I. Ramzy (Ed.). London: Hogarth Press and the Institute of Psycho-Analysis.

Winnicott, D. W. (1987). *The Spontaneous Gesture: Selected Letters of D. W. Winnicott.* F. R. Rodman (Ed.). Cambridge, MA: Harvard University Press.

Winnicott, D. W. (1988). *Human Nature.* (ed. C. Bollas, M. Davis, & R. Shepherd). London: Free Association Books

Winnicott, D. W., & Britton, C. (1944). The problem of homeless children. *The New Era in Home and School, 25:* 155–161.

Winnicott, D. W., & Britton, C. (1947). Residential management as treatment for difficult children: the evolution of a wartime hostels scheme. *Human Relations, 1:* 87–97.

Wolfenstein, M. (1957). *Disaster: A Psychological Study.* Glencoe, IL: Free Press and Falcon's Wing Press.

Wolff, P. H. (1966). *The Causes, Control and Organization of Behavior in the Neonate.* New York: International Universities Press.

Wood, C., Walker, A., & Yardley, R. (1979). Acceleration of the fetal heart rate. *American Journal of Obstetrics and Gynecology, 134:* 523–527.

INDEX